EDI[...]
JASON [...]

Birthday Poems

A CELEBRATION

THUNDER'S MOUTH PRESS NEW YORK

Birthday Poems

Published by
Thunder's Mouth Press
An Imprint of Avalon Publishing Group Incorporated
161 William St., 16th Floor
New York, NY 10038

Library of Congress Cataloging-in-Publication Data
is available for this title.

ISBN 1-56025-345-2

9 8 7 6 5 4 3 2 1

Printed in the United States of America
Distributed by Publishers Group West

contents

JASON SHINDER	INTRODUCTION	*xiii*
MILDRED J. HILL (1899–1916) & PATTY SMITH HILL (1868–1946)	Happy Birthday	*1*
	Happy Birthday to You A Short History of the Most Popular Song in the World	*3*
ROBERT FROST, 1874–1963	The Birthplace	*5*
WILLIAM CARLOS WILLIAMS, 1874–1963	To Be Recited To Flossie On Her Birthday	*6*
WALLACE STEVENS, 1879–1955	What We See Is What We Think	*7*
E.E. CUMMINGS, 1884–1962	65	*8*
EDNA ST. VINCENT MILLAY, 1892–1950	To Jesus on His Birthday	*9*
HORACE GREGORY, 1898–	Early April Morning	*10*
LANGSTON HUGHES, 1902–1967	Birth	*11*
KAY BOYLE, 1902–1992	For Marianne Moore's Birthday	*12*
EDWIN DENBY, 1903–	Birthday Sonnet	*13*
STANLEY KUNITZ, 1905–	Passing Through	*14*
ROBERT PENN WARREN, 1905–1989	To a Little Girl, One Year Old, In a Ruined Fortress	*16*

HELEN WOLFERT, 1910–	Birthdays	*25*
ROBERT FITZGERALD, 1910–	Silver Age Song	*26*
KENNETH PATCHEN, 1911–1972	What Splendid Birthdays	*27*
ELIZABETH BISHOP, 1911–1979	The Bight	*28*
PAUL GOODMAN, 1911–1972	Birthday Cake	*30*
JOSEPHINE JACOBSEN, 1911–	The Birthday Party	*31*
KARL SHAPIRO, 1913–2000	Moving In	*33*
ROBERT HAYDEN, 1913–1980	October	*35*
JOHN BERRYMAN, 1914–1972	Your Birthday in Wisconsin You Are 140	*37*
BARBARA HOWES, 1914–	To W.H. Auden on His Fiftieth Birthday	*38*
RANDALL JARRELL, 1914–1965	Aging	*39*
DAVID IGNATOW, 1914–2000	Birthday	*40*
WILLIAM STAFFORD, 1914–1993	The Only Card I Got on My Birthday Was from an Insurance Man	*41*
HILDA MORLEY, 1916–	Stefan—A Last Birthday Poem	*42*
JOHN CIARDI, 1916–	Poem for My Thirty-Ninth Birthday	*44*
ROBERT LOWELL, 1917–1977	Middle Age	*47*
MADELINE DEFRESS, 1919–	Birthday Poem	*48*
MAUD MEEHAN, 1920–	Gift for My Mother's 90th Birthday	*49*
MONA VAN DUYN, 1921–	Birthday Card for a Psychiatrist	*50*
JAMES DICKEY, 1923–	The Birthday Dream	*52*
ALAN DUGAN, 1923–	February Twelfth Birthday Statement	*54*
ANTHONY HECHT, 1923–	A Birthday Poem	*55*

JOHN LOGAN, 1923-	Lines on His Birthday	*58*
CAROLYN KIZER, 1924-	Poem for Your Birthday	*59*
EDWARD FIELD, 1924-	A Birthday Poem for My Little Sister	*61*
LISEL MUELLER, 1924-	For a Thirteenth Birthday	*63*
VASSAR MILLER, 1924-	On Approaching My Birthday	*66*
GERALD STERN, 1925	Birthday	*67*
KENNETH KOCH, 1925-	Poem for My 20th Birthday	*69*
DONALD JUSTICE, 1925-	A Birthday Candle	*70*
STANLEY MOSS, 1925-	Poem on My Birthday	*71*
PHILIP BOOTH, 1925-	Sixty-six	*73*
SAMUEL MENASHE, 1925-	On My Birthday	*75*
	49th Birthday Trip	*76*
JACK SPICER, 1925-1965	Five Words for Joe Dunn on His 22nd Birthday	*77*
MAXINE KUMIN, 1925-	Birthday Poem	*79*
ROBERT CREELEY, 1926-	A Birthday	*80*
A.R. AMMONS, 1926-2001	Birthday Poem to My Wife	*82*
FRANK O'HARA, 1926-1966	John Button Birthday	*83*
	To Canada (For Washington's Birthday)	*85*
	On a Birthday of Kenneth's	*86*
ALLEN GINSBERG, 1926-1997	Ode: My 24th Year	*87*
PHILLIP APPLEMAN, 1926-	Lighting Your Birthday Cake	*89*
W.S. MERWIN, 1927-	In the Winter of My Thirty-Eighth Year	*90*
GALWAY KINNELL, 1927-	First Day Of The Future	*91*

PETER DAVISON, 1927-	At Sixty	*92*
L.E. SISSMAN, 1928-1976	Safety at Forty	*93*
MAURICE KENNY, 1929-	Kaherawak's Birthday—July 28	*95*
	For Helene On Her 30th Birthday	*97*
GREGORY CORSO, 1930-2001	Writ on the Eve of My 32nd Birthday	*99*
	I am 25	*101*
MILLER WILLIAMS, 1930-	For Lucy, *On Her Birthday*	*102*
ETHERIDGE KNIGHT, 1931-1991	Birthday Poem	*103*
	A Poem for a Certain Lady on Her 33rd Birthday	*105*
SYLVIA PLATH, 1932-1966	A Birthday Present	*106*
JOHN UPDIKE, 1932-	Upon the Last Day of His Forty-Ninth Year	*109*
AUDRE LORDE, 1934-1992	A Birthday Memorial to Seventh Street	*110*
DIANE DIPRIMA, 1934-	April Fool Birthday Poem for Grandpa	*114*
SONIA SANCHEZ, 1934-	Poem at Thirty	*115*
TED BERRIGAN, 1934-1983	44th Birthday Evening, at Harris's	*116*
JOHN WEINERS, 1934-	My First Midnight 49th Birthday Supper	*117*
NELLE WONG, 1934-	Toward a 44th Birthday	*118*
JAY WRIGHT, 1934-	The Birthday	*119*
	A Non-Birthday Poem for My Father	*121*
JAMES SCHUYLER, 1935-1991	A Belated Birthday Poem	*126*
JUNE JORDAN, 1936-	DeLiza Come to London Town A Birthday Poem for Mark	*129*
LUCILLE CLIFTON, 1936-	The Thirty-Eight Year	*130*

DIANE WAKOSKI, 1937–	My Aunt Ella Meets the Buddha on His Birthday	*132*
JIM HARRISON, 1937–	Birthday	*136*
ALICIA OSTRIKER, 1937–	from *A Birthday Suite* (Happy Birthday)	*137*
MICHAEL S. HARPER, 1938–	Paul Laurence Dunbar	*138*
CHARLES SIMIC, 1938–	Birthday Star Atlas	*139*
ISHMAEL REED, 1938–	The Author Reflects on His 35th Birthday	*141*
STANLEY PLUMLY, 1939–	Birthday	*143*
FRANK BIDART, 1939–	Happy Birthday	*144*
STEPHEN DUNN, 1939–	Turning Fifty	*145*
ED OCHESTER, 1939–	On Frank O'Hara's Birthday	*147*
BRAD LETTHAUSER, 1940–	Small Waterfall: A Birthday Poem	*149*
JOHN LENNON, 1940–1980 & PAUL McCARTNEY, 1942–	Birthday	*151*
BOB DYLAN, 1941–	Forever Young	*152*
LOUISE GLUCK, 1941–	Birthday	*153*
PAUL ZWEIG, 1941–	Birth	*154*
SHARON OLDS, 1942–	June 24	*155*
	Birthday Poem for My Grandmother	*157*
MARILYN HACKER, 1942–	To Iva, Two-And-A-Half	*158*
RON PADGETT, 1942–	Poem for Joan Fagin on Her Birthday	*159*
LAURE-ANN BOSSELAAR, 1943–	For My Son	*160*
JAMES MOORE, 1943–	Preparing for Fifty	*161*

SUSAN MITCHELL, 1944–	Havana Birth	*162*
CAROL MUSKE, 1945–	Surprise	*165*
PHILIP SCHULTZ, 1945–	For My Birthday	*167*
BERNADETTE MAYER, 1945–	Birthday Sonnet for Grace	*168*
ANGELO VERGA, 1945–	My Brother's Birth Day	*169*
KEITH ALTHAUS, 1945–	Outlook	*170*
ANNE WALDMAN, 1945–	On Walt Whitman's Birthday	*171*
PATTI SMITH, 1946–	16 february	*172*
ANDREI CORDESCU, 1946–	Imported Days	*173*
COLLEEN ELROY, 1946–	At 102, Romance Comes Once A Year	*174*
CHARLIE SMITH, 1947–	Mother at Eighty	*176*
CLEOPATRA MATHIS, 1947–	On a Shared Birthday	*177*
MICHAEL BURKARD, 1947–	A Birthday Story	*179*
GREGORY ORR, 1947–	Nicole at Thirteen	*181*
PETER VIERECK, 1948–	Fiftieth Birthday	*182*
DAVID LEHMAN, 1948–	June 11	*183*
EILEEN MYLES, 1949–	December 9th	*184*
E. ETHELBERT MILLER, 1950–	Enid at 70	*185*
MELVIN DIXON, 1950–1992	Turning Forty in the 90s	*186*
JIM CARROLL, 1951–	Poem on My Son's Birthday	*187*
JIMMY SANTIAGO BACA, 1952–	A Good Day	*188*
RITA DOVE, 1952–	Turning Thirty, I Contemplate Students Bicycling Home	*190*
	Wingfoot Lake	*191*

KEVIN PILKINGTON, 1953– | Birthday | *193*
M.L. LIEBLER, 1953– | Birthday Dream | *195*
DENIS COOPER, 1953– | John Kennedy Jr. at Twenty-One | *196*
For My Birthday | *198*
DEBRA NYSTROM, 1954– | Relic | *199*
LIZ ROSENBERG, 1955– | The Birthday Party | *200*
FRANZ WRIGHT, 1955– | Birthday | *201*
SOPHIE CABOT BLACK, 1958– | On the Birthday | *202*
JUANITA BRUNK, 1958– | Birthday Poem | *203*
ELYSE PASCHEN, 1959– | Birth Day | *204*
RAY GONZALEZ, 1959– | Birthday | *205*
DEBORAH GARRISON, 1965– | She Thinks of Him on Her Birthday | *207*
SILVIA CURBELO, 1966– | Birthday Song | *208*

INDEX *211*

PERMISSIONS *215*

ABOUT THE EDITOR *225*

*Although every attempt was made to confirm the year of birth of each poet, there is the possibility that one or two dates may not be accurate.

introduction

MANY DAYS CAN BE uneventful, forgotten, fleeting—but the anniversary of the day of our birth is often full of anticipation, excitement, and sometimes, passion and surprise. For many of us, birthdays not only conjure up powerful feelings, but, as we grow older, memories of previous birthday surface, good and not-so-good, especially those from childhood. Boxes wrapped in colorful paper, chocolate candy inside a chocolate ice-cream cake with candles lighting up a room with the familiar faces of loved ones—these are just some of the images we might be fortunate enough to conjure up.

For everyone, including our nation's poets, the expectation that exciting moments, gifts, and memories will surface on one's birthday seems almost hereditary—as if there were birthday genes floating somewhere in the blood. In e.e. cummings' poem *65*, the poet confirms this seemingly human trait:

I who have died am alive again today
and this is the sun's birthyear; this is the birth
day of life and of love and wings: and the gay
great happening illimitably earth.

For some, of course, birthdays are not always approached only with excitement and anticipation. Instead, birthdays can sometimes recall hours thick with difficult self-reflection, walking aimlessly, hands in pockets in the middle of town, in the middle of the night. Full of great expectations, birthdays can fall short, coming down upon us with a loud, or not-so-loud, thud. Rita Dove contemplates her 30th birthday with a sense of such disconnectness and disappointment.

How private
the complaint of these
green hills.

The excitement and despair associated with birthdays, the generosity of wishing others and oneself secret, eternal wishes, the transformative power of seeing one's loved ones gathered together in one place; the magic and mystery of rituals such as lighting candles, eating cake, and singing; the helpless annual meditations on the value and meaning of life—these are just a few of the many and various catalysts for the birthday poems in this collection.

II

WALT Whitman wondered if animals were as obsessed as people were with remembering, and recording, their birth and existence:

They do not sweat and whine about their condition.
They do not lie awake in the dark and weep for their sins.
They do not make us such discussing their duty to God.

Animals may call out to each other across empty fields and valleys—loud, upward-whining wails—on the day of birth of their offspring. Yet there is no indication that any other animals besides humans spend so much time documenting and celebrating the occasion. As with all animals, the day of birth opens up the lived life. Yet the memory of that day seems to help keep alive the range of life's possibilities for humans.

Such fascination with the anniversary of our birth was not always the case. Our earliest ancestors first applied this most human characteristic to their kings and Gods. One of the first birthdays ever recorded was found on a Rosetta stone, inscribed by priests in the second century B.C. The inscription found on the stone celebrated the life of Ptolemy V.

Ptolemy V, the ever living, the beloved of Ptah, the son of two Brother-Gods, was born on the fifth day of the month DIOS, and this day was, in consequence, the beginning of great prosperity and happiness of all living men and women.

A symbol that followed the inscription has been translated as "the beginning of much happiness" or "the opening of the year." The inscription, and the symbol, make it clear that the birth of Kings were viewed as the beginning of great things for all—so much, in fact, that it would have been a failure of the ruling class and their subjects not to jot down everything about their birth and to celebrate it.

Among the dangerous hardships (and spirits) of the earth, many believed, in fact, that only a proper celebration of the birthdays of the ruling class could keep the evil spirits away. After all, what better time for the devil to demonstrate its power than on the anniversary of the day life was given? To ensure the evil spirits were kept away, the birthday person was surrounded by friends and relatives whose good wishes, gifts, and very presences, were intended to sniff out any lurking bad spirits—not to mention sickness, starvation and poverty. And the earlier on the anniversary of one's birth that friends gathered, the greater impact their good wishes would have.

And though many Kings and Queens scoffed at the power of evil spirits against their own power, they were determined to have as many people around them on their birthday as was possible. The Bible speaks of the birthday of the great Egyptian sovereign Pharaoh, King of Egypt (Genesis 40), who apparently celebrated his birthdays by giving a household feasts in which everyone was ordered to appear—the more people the more protection against evil. It was said that prisoners were released from jail to join the celebration, making it as large a gathering as possible.

III

THE need to protect oneself against evil on the anniversary of one's birth was soon everyone's concern, from those with wealth and power to those without. The Greek Historian, Herodotus, described this new tradition:

It is our custom to honor our birthday above all other days, and on this day to furnish our table in a more plentiful manner than at other times. The rich may produce an ox, horse, camel . . . but the poor may produce camel.

The Greeks, in fact, came to believe that the celebration of one's birth was not only necessary to protect oneself against the devil, but a way to invite an angel to watch over one's life.

The Greeks, and others, called this protective angel or spirit one's "genius." And it remains one of the first meanings of the word genius, that of "a particular spirit of an age." The more familiar definition of the word, that "of having mental capacity and inventive ability" was shaped, in part, by the rituals surrounding the celebration of birthdays and one's ability to protect oneself, and others, from ruin.

Within this drama, the meaning of birthdays grew more and more critical. On his birthdays, Pharaoh began to listen intently to fortune tellers and astrologers. On one occasion, he is said to have hanged his chief baker on the basis that a dream of the baker's predicted a death near the time of his birthday.

The power of celebrating our birth was not shared by all. Father Origen of Alexandra was so concerned about the temptations of the flesh on such occasions that he emasculated himself. In a homily on Leviticus he wrote:

None of the saints can be found who ever held a feast or a banquet upon his birthday, or rejoiced on the day when his son or daughter was born. But sinners rejoice and make merry on such days. . . . The saints not only neglect to mark the day of their birth with festivity, but also, filled with the Holy Ghost, they curse this day!

When we look back, however, at the origins of the celebration of the day of our birth, it is the festivity and celebration that continues to grow and mark the day. So enthralled with the celebration of birth, many today continue to celebrate the anniversary of a person's birth even after a person's death.

My sister, in fact, told me about a time when she and my six-year-old niece were talking about our father living in Heaven, full of flowers and wonderful fragrances. My niece turned abruptly toward my sister, and asked why they never celebrated his birthday. "It's still his birthday even if he's in heaven," she declared. After all, birthdays don't die with the person. Or do they? Now each May 16th my sister and niece take time to light a candle and send my father in Heaven birthday wishes.

Birthday Poems is the first book to represent poetry on birthdays written exclusively by American poets in the last century. The poets are arranged chronologically, beginning with the American authors of the world's most popular song-poem, *Happy Birthday To You*. Although a timeless song, one that seems to have always been with us, *Happy Birthday to You*, was, in fact, written by two sisters born at the end of the 19th century. I hope the chronological order will allow the reader the opportunity to trace the development of our poets' approach to birthdays, and of the birthday poem itself.

With more than 135 poets, many of whom of our country's most influential and celebrated, I also hope the book will illuminate the subtle and dramatic changes in form and content, as well as the constants of passion and honesty, that distinguish our rich and dynamic twentieth (and now twenty-first) century of American poetry.

The poems I have selected represent a small part of a larger and rapidly growing body of work. Because of space constraints, I have limited the collection to shorter birthday poems and to sections, where appropriate, of longer poems on the subject. I have also included in the book an annotation on the short history of the song-poem, *Happy Birthday to You*, to illuminate the rather curious history of the world's most popular writing about birthdays, and the world's most popular song.

I am grateful to the many people who provided new insights into the poems I was considering for this collection, and to the many poets, editors, teachers, and friends, who brought birthday poems to my attention. Special thanks, first and foremost, to the poet Angelo Verga, the book's senior research and editorial assistant, for his outstanding work and attention. Thanks also to Neil Ortenberg and Dan O'Connor from Thunder's Mouth press for their ongoing support and critical insights. Thanks too to Katie Adams, Sophie Cabot Black, Laurel Blossom, Ken Brecher, Lucie Brock-Brodio, Tony Hoagland, Marie Howe, Carla

Israelson, Sarah Ann Johnson, Sheila Murphy, Carol Stutz and Stanley Kunitz.

Thanks, finally, to the poets for their poems and to the people who granted permission to reprint them.

for everyone

what thou lovest well remains, the rest is dross

what thou lov'st well shall not be reft from thee

what thou lov'st well is thy true heritage

EZRA POUND

Birthday Poems

Happy Birthday

Happy birthday to you.
Happy birthday to you.
Happy birthday, dear __________.
Happy birthday to you!

The Happy Birthday Party Song

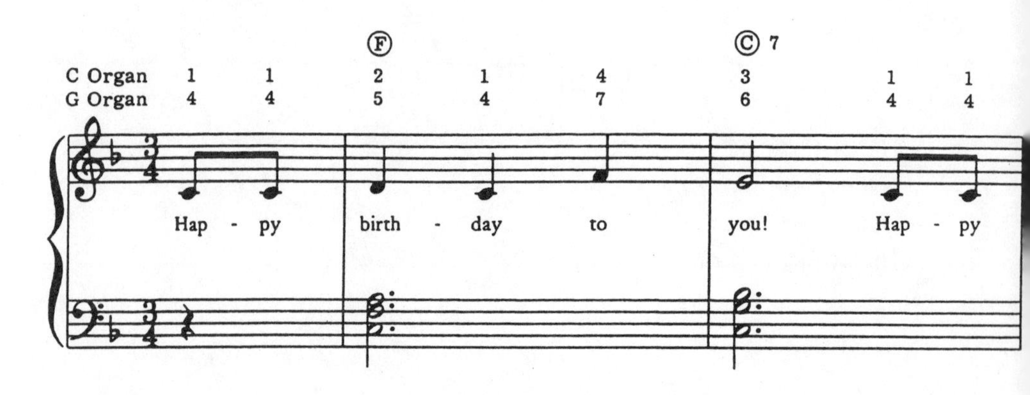

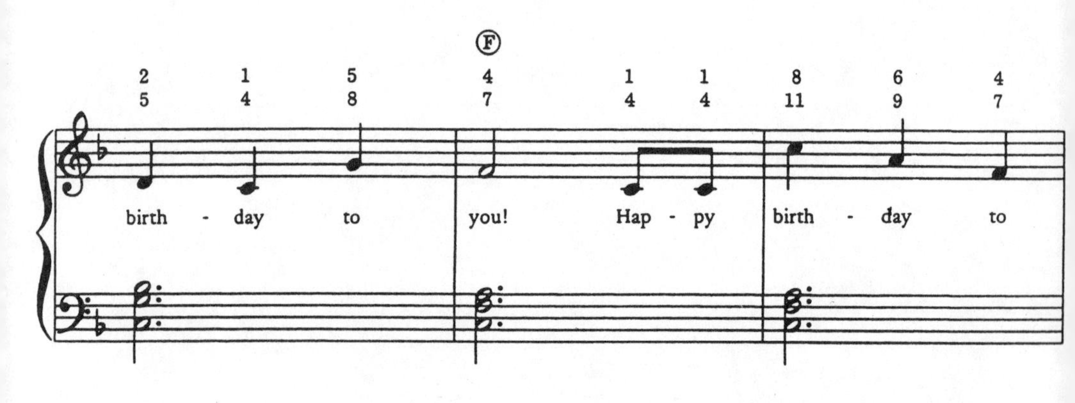

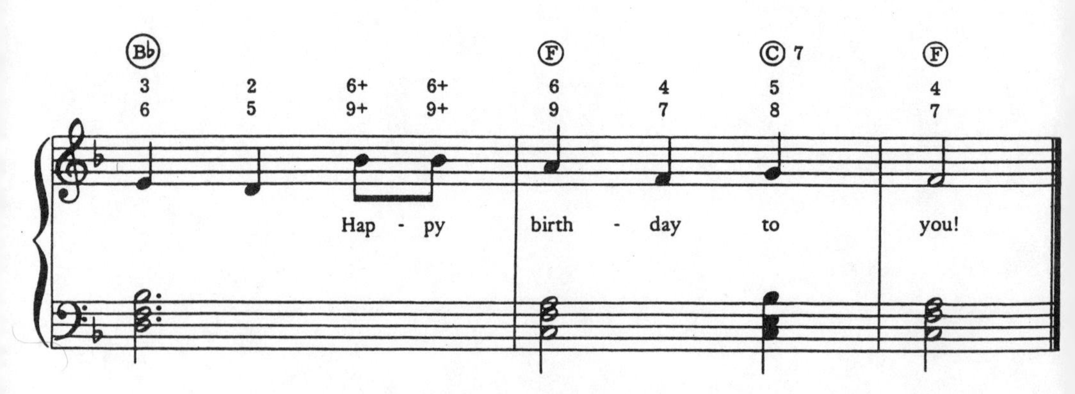

Happy Birthday To You:

A Short History of the Most Popular Song in the World

Happy Birthday to You may seem as if it belongs to everyone, but the song was actually authored by two sisters only a hundred or so years ago and is still under copyright.

Now the most popular song in the world, *Happy Birthday To You,* (according to the Guinness Book of World Records), was written in 1893 in the town of Louisville, KY.

There, two middle-aged sisters, both kindergarten and Sunday school teachers, Patty Hill and Mildred J. Hill decided to write a book of "song stories" for their students. The book entitled *Song Stories for The Sunday School,* was distributed in the spring of 1893 and contained a most melodious lyric/nursery rhyme entitled "Good Morning To You."

Good morning to you,
Good morning to you,
Good morning, dear Children,
Good morning to all

Mildred H. Hill wrote the music, and her sister, Patti, wrote the words.

The circumstances surrounding the changing of the words *Good Morning to All to Happy Birthday to You* are sketchy. For reasons yet unclear, the Hill Sisters added the birthday words in the early 1900s. The first published account of the song appeared in 1924, without any mention of the Hill Sisters, in the book *Harvest Hymns,* edited by Robert H. Coleman. It is likely that Coleman came upon the song in his travels as a publisher.

The song then found its way to Broadway, where it was sung in the musical, *As Thousands Cheer*. Once again the song was used without the permission of the Hill Sisters, and they sued the producer of the show, Sam H. Harris. On August 13, 1934, the *NY Times* reported the lawsuit, and in December the paper reported that the Hill Sisters won their case—at which point the song received copyright protection for 75 years. Since then ownership of the song has changed several times, with the Hill sisters and their heirs receiving the author's shares of the gross profits. Today the song is owned by Warner Communications until the song's copyright expires in 2010. (Because there are few new recordings of the song, annual royalties are not very high.)

How did the lyric *Happy Birthday To You* become so popular? No one really knows but its appearance in several early movies, and its being programmed with musical boxes, toys and even watches, accounted for some of its now worldwide popularity.

The Birthplace

Here further up the mountain slope
Than there was ever any hope,
My father built, enclosed a spring,
Strung chains of wall round everything,
Subdued the growth of earth to grass,
And brought our various lives to pass.
A dozen girls and boys we were.
The mountain seemed to like the stir,
And made of us a little while—
With always something in her smile.
Today she wouldn't know our name.
(No girl's, of course, has stayed the same.)
The mountain pushed us off her knees.
And now her lap is full of trees.

To Be Recited to Flossie on Her Birthday

Let him who may
among the continuing lines
seek out

that tortured constancy
affirms
where I persist

let me say
across cross purposes
that the flower bloomed

struggling to assert itself
simply under
the conflicting lights

you will believe me
a rose
to the end of time

What We See Is What We Think

At twelve, the disintegration of afternoon
Began, the return to phantomerei, if not
To phantoms. Till then, it had been the other way:

One imagined the violet trees but the trees stood green,
At twelve, as green as ever they would be.
The sky was blue beyond the vaultiest phrase.

Twelve meant as much as: the end of normal time,
Straight up, an élan without harrowing,
The imprescriptible zenith, free of harangue,

Twelve and the first gray second after, a kind
Of violet gray, a green violet, a thread
To weave a shadow's leg or sleeve, a scrawl

On the pedestal, an ambitious page dog-eared
At the upper right, a pyramid with one side
Like a spectral cut in its perception, a tilt

And its tawny caricature and tawny life,
Another thought, the paramount ado . . .
Since what we think is never what we se.

65

i thank You God for most this amazing
day:for the leaping greenly spirits of trees
and a blue true dream of sky;and for everything
which is natural which is infinite which is yes

(i who have died am alive again today,
and this is the sun's birthday;this is the birth
day of life and of love and wings:and of the gay
great happening illimitably earth)

how should tasting touching hearing seeing
breathing any—lifted from the no
of all nothing—human merely being
doubt unimaginable You?

(now the ears of my ears awake and
now the eyes of my eyes are opened)

To Jesus on His Birthday

For this your mother sweated in the cold,
For this you bled upon the bitter tree:
A yard of tinsel ribbon bought and sold;
A paper wreath; a day at home for me.
The merry bells ring out, the people kneel;
Up goes the man of God before the crowd;
With voice of honey and with eyes of steel
He drones your humble gospel to the proud.
Nobody listens. Less than the wind that blows
Are all your words to us you died to save.
O Prince of Peace! O Sharon's dewy Rose!
How mute you lie within your vaulted grave.
The stone the angel rolled away with tears
Is back upon your mouth these thousand years.

Early April Morning

This is the day that I began.
                                        This is new year's
in the terse calendar that opens with my name:
April and south winds in the sky repeat the same
rhythm, and the indigenous body hears
spring at morning waking the same trees that always
bear the sun on slender branches that somehow rise
out of dark streets down-circling nightward
                                                    and our eyes
turn from roots gathered and unwinding
                                              under doors and hallways.

It is not the season, but the inevitable
return of seasons that unshapes the days, the hours
caught in the mind, and builds them new again:
                                                         flowers
and grass covering a ruined city.
                                          From wild Aquarius
into waiting Aries, I retrace the day my breath
first issued toward my last decade:
let choir, spire, earth, O Trinity, answer death.

Birth

Oh, fields of wonder
Out of which
Stars are born,
And moon and sun
And me as well,
Like stroke
Of lightning
In the night
Some mark
To make
Some word
To tell.

For Marianne Moore's Birthday

November 15, 1967

I wish you triumphs that are yours already,
And also wish to say whatever I have done
Has been in admiration (imitation even)
Of all you marvelously proliferate. Once someone
Turned to me and said in lowered voice (because you too were in the
    room)
That William Carlos Williams gave to you at sight that
Singular esteem known by no other name save love. These words were
Spoken perhaps a half century ago
(In Monroe Wheeler's Eastside flat) when you
Wore amber braids around your head. And now,
As then, I cannot write this book or that
Without you. You have always been
Nightingale, baseball fan, librarian of my visions,
Poised on a moving ladder in the sun.

[1970]

Birthday Sonnet

A Postcard

Elaine, Nini, Sylvia, Marjorie, Theda,
Each sends you happy wishes for your birthday,
Red and black Frances, Frannie, and Almavida,
Louise, gay Germaine too who is far away,
Kind Maggie, and Pit, Martha who prays gladly,
Jeannie, Ruth, Ernestine, Anne, Billie Holiday,
Husky Patsy, Ilse they love so madly,
And straightforward Teddy—Dear Rudy, they all say.
And then Victor, and Bill, and Walter the mild,
And Frank, David, John, Aaron, Paul, Harry and
Virgil, the Photoleague, Oliver, Ebbie wild,
I and Gankie and the Shoe-man shake your hand.
Marieli and Susan come running at the end
And all of us send our love to you, our friend.

Passing Through

—on my seventy-ninth birthday

Nobody in the widow's household
ever celebrated anniversaries.
In the secrecy of my room
I would not admit I cared
that my friends were given parties.
Before I left town for school
my birthday went up in smoke
in a fire at City Hall that gutted
the Department of Vital Statistics.
If it weren't for a census report
of a five-year-old White Male
sharing my mother's address
at the Green Street tenement in Worcester
I'd have no documentary proof
that I exist. You are the first,
my dear, to bully me
into these festive occasions.

Sometimes, you say, I wear
an abstracted look that drives you
up the wall, as though it signified
distress or disaffection.
Don't take it so to heart.
Maybe I enjoy not-being as much
as being who I am. Maybe
it's time for me to practice
growing old. The way I look
at it, I'm passing through a phase:
gradually I'm changing to a word.

Whatever you choose to claim
of me is always yours;
nothing is truly mine
except my name. I only
borrowed this dust.

To a Little Girl, One Year Old, In a Ruined Fortress

To Rosanna

I
Sirocco

To a place of ruined stone we brought you, and sea-reaches.
Rocca: fortress, hawk-heel, lion-paw, clamped on a hill.
A hill, no. On a sea cliff, and crag-cocked, the embrasures
commanding the beaches,
Range easy, with most fastidious mathematic and skill.

Philipus me fecit: he of Spain, the black-browed, the anguished,
For whom nothing prospered, though he loved God.
His arms, a great scutcheon of stone, once over the drawbridge,
have languished
Now long in the moat, under garbage; at moat-brink, rosemary
with blue, thistle with gold bloom, nod.

Sun blaze and cloud tatter, now the sirocco, the dust swirl is swirled
Over the bay face, mounts air like gold gauze whirled; it traverses
the blaze-blue of water.
We have brought you where geometry of a military rigor survives
its own ruined world,
And sun regilds your gilt hair, in the midst of your laughter.

Rosemary, thistle, clutch stone. Far hangs Giannutri in blue air.
Far to that blueness the heart aches,
And on the exposed approaches the last gold of gorse bloom, in the
sirocco, shakes.

II
Gull's Cry

White goose by palm tree, palm ragged, among stones the white oleander,
And the she-goat, brown, under pink oleanders, waits.
I do not think that anything in the world will move, not goat, not gander.
Goat droppings are fresh in the hot dust; not yet the beetle; the sun beats,

And under blue shade of the mountain, over blue-braiding sea-shadow,
The gull hangs white; whiter than white against the mountain-mass,
The gull extends motionless on a shelf of air, on the substance of shadow.
The gull, at an eye-blink, will, into the astonishing statement of sun, pass.

All night, next door, the defective child cried; now squats in the dust
where the lizard goes.
The wife of the *gobbo* sits under vine leaves, she suffers, her eyes glare.
The engaged ones sit in the privacy of bemusement, heads bent: the
classic pose.
Let the beetle work, the gull comment the irrelevant anguish of air,

But at your laughter let the molecular dance of the stone-dark
glimmer like joy in the stone's dream,
And in that moment of possibility, let *gobbo, gobbo's* wife, and us, and all,
take hands and sing: *redeem, redeem!*

III
The Child Next Door

The child next door is defective because the mother,
Seven brats already in that purlieu of dirt,
Took a pill, or did something to herself she thought would not hurt,
But it did, and no good, for there came this monstrous other.

The sister is twelve. Is beautiful like a saint.
Sits with the monster all day, with pure love, calm eyes.
Has taught it a trick, to make *ciao*, Italian-wise.
It crooks hand in that greeting. She smiles her smile without taint.

* * *

I come, and her triptych beauty and joy stir hate
—Is it hate?—in my heart. Fool, doesn't she know that the process
Is not that joyous or simple, to bless, or unbless,
The malfeasance of nature or the filth of fate?

Can it bind or loose, that beauty in that kind,
Beauty of benediction? We must trust our hope to prevail
That heart-joy in beauty be wisdom, before beauty fail
And be gathered like air in the ruck of the world's wind!

I think of your goldness, of joy, but how empires grind, stars are hurled.
I smile stiff, saying *ciao*, saying *ciao*, and think: *This is the world.*

IV
The Flower

Above the beach, the vineyard
Terrace breaks to the seaward
Drop, where the cliffs fail
To a clutter of manganese shale.
Some is purple, some powdery-pale.
But the black lava-chunks stand off
The sea's grind, or indolent chuff.
The lava will withstand
The sea's beat, or insinuant hand,
And protect our patch of sand.

It is late. The path from the beach
Crawls up. I take you. We reach
The vineyard, and at that path angle
The hedge obtrudes a tangle
Of leaf and green bulge and a wrangle
Bee-drowsy and blowsy with white bloom,
Scarcely giving the passer-by room.

We know that the blossomy mass
Will brush our heads as we pass,
And at knee there's gold gorse and blue clover,
And at ankle, blue *malva* all over—
Plus plants I don't recognize
With my non-botanical eyes.
We approach, but before we get there,
If no breeze stirs that green lair,
The scent and sun-honey of air
Is too sweet comfortably to bear.

I carry you up the hill.
In my arms you are still.
We approach your special place,
and I am watching your face
To see the sweet puzzlement grow,
And then recognition glow.
Recognition explodes in delight.
You leap like spray, or like light.
Despite my arm's tightness,
You leap in gold-glitter and brightness.
You leap like a fish-flash in bright air,
And reach out. Yes, I'm well aware
That this is the spot, and hour,
For you to demand your flower.

When first we came this way
Up from the beach, that day
That seems now so long ago,
We moved bemused and slow
In the season's pulse and flow.
Bemused with sea, and slow
With June heat and perfume,
We paused here, and plucked you a bloom.
So here you always demand
Your flower to hold in your hand,

* * *

And the flower must be white,
For you have your own ways to compel
Observance of this ritual.
You hold it and sing with delight.
And your mother, for our own delight,
Picks one of the blue flowers there,
To put in your yellow hair.
That done, we go in our way
Up the hill, toward the end of the day.

But the season has thinned out.
From the bay edge below, the shout
Of a late bather reaches our ear,
Coming to the vineyard here
By more than distance thinned.
The bay is in shadow, the wind
Nags the shore to white.
The mountain prepares the night.

By the vineyard we have found
No bloom worthily white,
And the few we have found
Not disintegrated to the ground
Are by season and sea-salt browned.
We give the best one to you.
It is ruined, but will have to do.
Somewhat better the blue blossoms fare.
So we find one for your hair,
And you sing as though human need
Were not for perfection. We proceed
Past floss-borne or sloughed-off seed,
Past curled leaf and dry pod,
And the blue blossom will nod
With your head's drowsy gold nod.

Let all seasons pace their power,
As this has paced to this hour.
Let season and season devise
Their possibilities.
Let the future reassess
All past joy, and past distress,
Till we know Time's deep intent,
And the last integument
Of the past shall be rent
To show how all things bent
Their energies to that hour
When you first demanded your flower.

Yes, in that image let
Both past and future forget,
In clasped communal ease,
Their brute identities.

The path lifts up ahead
To the *rocca*, supper, bed.
We move in the mountain's shade.
The mountain is at our back.
But ahead, climbs the coast-cliff track.
The valley between is dim.
Ahead, on the cliff rim,
The *rocca* clasps its height.
It accepts the incipient night.

Just once we look back.
On sunset, a white gull is black.
It hangs over the mountain crest.
It hangs on that saffron west.
It makes its outcry.
It slides down the sky.

East now, it catches the light.
Its black has gone again white,
And over the *rocca's* height
It gleams in the last light.

* * *

Now it sinks from our sight.
Beyond the cliff is night.

It sank on unruffled wing.
We hear the sea rustling.

V
Colder Fire

It rained toward day. The morning came sad and white
With silver of sea-sadness and defection of season.
Our joys and convictions are sure, but in that wan light
We moved—your mother and I—in muteness of spirit past logical reason.

Now sun, afternoon, and again summer-glitter on sea.
As you to a bright toy, the heart leaps. The heart unlocks
Joy, though we know, shamefaced, the heart's weather should not be
Merely a reflex to a solstice, or sport of some aggrieved equinox.

No, the heart should be steadfast: I know that.
And I sit in the late-sunny lee of the watch-house,
At the fortress point, you on my knee now, and the late
White butterflies over gold thistle conduct their ritual carouse.

In whisperless carnival, in vehemence of gossamer,
Pale ghosts of pale passions of air, the white wings weave.
In tingle and tangle of arabesque, they mount light, pair by pair,
As though that tall light were eternal indeed, not merely the summer's
reprieve.

You leap on my knee, you explain at the sun-stung gyration.
And the upper air stirs, as though the vast stillness of sky
Had stirred in its sunlit sleep and made suspiration,
A luxurious langour of breath, as after love, there is a sigh.

But enough, for the highest sun-scintillant pair are gone
Seaward, past rampart and cliff borne, over blue sea-gleam.
Close to my chair, to a thistle, a butterfly sinks now, flight done.
By the gold bloom of thistle, white wings pulse under the sky's dream.

The sky's dream is enormous, I lift up my eyes.
In sunlight a tatter of mist clings high on the mountain-mass.
The mountain is under the sky, and there the gray scarps rise
Past paths where on their appointed occasions men climb, and pass.

Past grain-patch, last apron of vineyard, last terrace of olive,
Past chestnut, past cork grove, where the last carts can go,
Past camp of the charcoal maker, where coals glow in the black hive,
The scarps, gray, rise up. Above them is that place I know.

The pines are there, they are large, in a deep recess—
Shelf above scarp, enclave of rock, a glade
Benched and withdrawn in the mountain-mass, under the peak's duress.
We came there—your mother and I—and rested in that severe shade.

Pine-blackness mist-tangled, the peak black above: the glade gives
On the empty threshold of air, the hawk-hung delight
Of distance unspooled and bright space spilled—ah, the heart thrives!
We stood in that shade and saw sea and land lift in the far light.

Now the butterflies dance, time-tattered and disarrayed.
I watch them. I think how above that far scarp's sunlit wall
Mist threads in silence the darkness of boughs, and in that shade
Condensed moisture gathers at a needle-tip. It glitters, will fall.

I cannot interpret for you this collocation
Of memories. You will live your own life, and contrive
The language of your own heart, but let that conversation,
In the last analysis, be always of whatever truth you would live.

* * *

For fire flames but in the heart of a colder fire.
All voice is but echo caught from a soundless voice.
Height is not deprivation of valley, nor defect of desire,
But defines, for the fortunate, that joy in which all joys should rejoice.

Birthdays

Under the revolution of the moon,
the morning to morning of the sun,
let not my mother be forgotten;
who on the soonest minute
of a ripe and riotous January dawn,
became a heretic;
bore a green berry daughter,
unfit to be born;
committed a sin
against evolution.

Under the seedless burial stone
let not my father be forgotten;
who hailing me,
so minutely unfit
for my new dwelling,
(where wit served often
as milk, as bread and mead,)
remained as ever the able provider,
and ably said,
"You could thread a needle with this baby."

Nor forget
the skuttle of black suns
or the black polish dandy of the kitchen
with the four apple cheeks,
who blew his fruits into the air,
fanned them forward, fanned them backward,
to an orchard in the kitchen, a vineyard in the bedroom;
while the blizzard
ghoulish at every crack
whinnied and whined, "Jut let me in!"

Silver Age Song

DROPLET in the western air,
Flashing tremulously fair,

Couching star, this evening shine
On velleities like mine.

Bless all bridals long foregone;
Wake us not this night alone.

Wild beasts in their lairs abide;
Grant us gentle, side by side.

Underground lie grisly men;
Let each swan pair with his pen.

Child of heaven and the sea,
Grace our mortal venery.

What Splendid Birthdays

The ears of the forest
Twitch in the sun
Flies of cloud
Are shaken off so carefully

See, they alight again

In confident purity
And their wings seem to rest
Against the sky like
Candleflames painted on a cake

Deer in the sunglow

Green ears
Twitching sleepily in the warmth
Of
A peaceful summer's afternoon
Later . . . the herd stirs awake
Antlers purpling
And the first match

Touches the darkling candelabra

The Bight

[On my birthday]

At low tide like this how sheer the water is.
White, crumbling ribs of marl protrude and glare
and the boats are dry, the pilings dry as matches.
Absorbing, rather than being absorbed,
the water in the bight doesn't wet anything,
the color of the gas flame turned as low as possible.
One can smell it turning to gas; if one were Baudelaire
one could probably hear it turning to marimba music.
The little ocher dredge at work off the end of the dock
already plays the dry perfectly off-beat claves.
The birds are outsize. Pelicans crash
into this peculiar gas unnecessarily hard,
it seems to me, like pickaxes,
rarely coming up with anything to show for it,
and going off with humorous elbowings.
Black-and-white man-of-war birds soar
on impalpable drafts
and open their tails like scissors on the curves
or tense them like wishbones, till they tremble.
The frowsy sponge boats keep coming in
with the obliging air of retrievers,
bristling with jackstraw gaffs and hooks
and decorated with bobbles of sponges.
There is a fence of chicken wire along the dock
where, glinting like little plowshares,
the blue-gray shark tails are hung up to dry
for the Chinese-restaurant trade.
Some of the little white boats are still piled up
against each other, or lie on their sides, stove in,

and not yet salvaged, if they ever will be, from the last bad storm,
like torn-open, unanswered letters.
The bight is littered with old correspondences.
Click. Click. Goes the dredge,
And brings up a dripping jawful of marl.
All the untidy activity continues,
awful but cheerful.

Birthday Cake

Now isn't it time
when the candles on the icing
are one two too many
too many to blow out
too many to count too many
isn't it time to give up this ritual?

although the fiery crown
fluttering on the chocolate
and through the darkened room advancing
is still the most loveliest sight
among our savage folk
that have few festivals.

But the thicket is too hot and thick
and isn't it time, isn't it time
when the fires are too many
to eat the fire and not the cake
and drip the fires from my teeth
as once I had my hot hot youth.

The Birthday Party

The sounds are the sea, breaking out of sight,
and down the green slope the children's voices
that celebrate the fact of being eight.

One too few chairs are for desperate forces:
when the music hushes, the children drop
into their arms, except for one caught by choices.

In a circle gallops the shrinking crop
to leave a single sitter in hubris
when the adult finger tells them: stop.

There is a treasure, somewhere easy to miss.
In the blooms? by the pineapple-palms' bark?
somewhere, hidden, the shape of bliss.

Onto the pitted sand comes highwater mark.
Waves older than eight begin a retreat;
they will come, the children gone, the slope dark.

One of the gifts was a year, complete.
There will be others: those not eight
will come to be eight, bar a dire defeat.

On the green grass there is a delicate
change; there is a change in the sun
though certainly it is not truly late,

and still caught up in the scary fun,
like a muddle of flowers blown around.
For treasure, for triumph, the children run

and the wind carries the steady pound,
and salty weight that falls, and dies,
and falls. The wind carries the sound

of the children's light high clear cries.

Moving In

I wish you for your birthday as you are,
Inherently happy,
The little girl always shining out of your face
And the woman standing her ground.

Wish you the seldom oceanic earthquake
Which shatters your gaze
Against some previous interior past
And rights you.

Wish you your honest normal as a tree
Confounding the caws of intellectuals.
When I zip your dress I kiss you on the neck.
A talisman in honor of your pride.

When I hold your head in my hands
It is as of the roundness of Columbus
Thinking the world, "my hands capable of
Designing the earthly sphere."

Your fingers on the piano keys
Or the typewriter keys or on my face
Write identical transcriptions.
Nothing you do is lost in translation.

I am delighted that you loathe Christmas.
I feel the same way about Communism.
Let us live in the best possible house,
Selfish and true.

May the Verdi *Requiem* continue to knock you out
As it does me; fashionable protest art
Continue to infuriate your heart
And make you spill your drink.

Now ideology has had its day
Nothing is more important than your birthday.
Let us have a solid roof over our head
And bless one another.

October

I

October—
its plangency, its glow

as of words in
the poet's mind,

as of God in
the saint's.

II

I wept for your mother
in her pain, wept in
my joy when you were
born,
            Maia,
that October morning.
We named you
for a star a star-like
poem sang.
                              I write this
for your birthday
and say I love you
and say October
like the phoenix sings you.

III

This chiming
and tolling
          of lion
and phoenix
and chimera
          colors.
This huntsman's
horn, sounding
          mort for
quarry fleeing
through mirrors
          of burning
into deathless
          dying.

IV

Rockweight
of surprising snow

crushed
the October trees,

broke
branches that

crashing set
the snow on fire.

Your Birthday in Wisconsin You Are 140

'One of the wits of the school' your chum would say—
Hot diggity!—What the *hell* went wrong for you,
Miss Emily,—besides the 'pure & terrible' Congressman
your paralyzing papa,—and Mr Humphrey's dying
& Benjamin's the other reader? . . .

Fantastic at 32 outpour, uproar, 'terror
since September, I could tell to none'
after your 'Master' moved his family West
and timidly to Mr Higginson:
'say if my verse is alive.'

Now you wore only white, now you did not appear,
till frantic 50 when you hurled your heart
down before Otis, who would none of it
thro' five years for 'Squire Dickinson's cracked daughter'
awful by months, by hours . . .

Well. Thursday afternoon, I'm in W———
drinking your ditties, and (dear) *they* are *alive*,—
more so than (bless her) Mrs F who teaches
farmers' red daughters & their beaux *my* ditties
and yours & yours & yours!
Hot diggity!

To W. H. Auden on His Fiftieth Birthday

Books collide—
Or books in a library do:
Marlowe by Charlotte Mew,
Sir Horace Walpole by Hugh;
The most unlikely writers stand shoulder to shoulder;
One studies incongruity as one grows older.

Symbols collide—
Signs of the zodiac
Range the celestial track,
Pisces has now swung back
Into the lead: we learn to recognize
Each fleck for what it is in our mackerel skies.

Ideas collide—
As words in a poem can.
The poet, Promethean,
Strikes fire in a single line,
Form glows in the far reaches of his brain;
Poets who travel will come home again.

Feeling collides—
Lying for years in wait,
May grope or hesitate.
Now let us celebrate
Feeling, ideas, symbols, books which can
Meet with greatness here within one man.

Aging

I wake, but before I know it is done,
The day, I sleep. And of days like these the years,
A life is made. I nod, consenting to my life.
. . . But who can live in these quick-passing hours?
I need to find again, to make a life,
A child's Sunday afternoon, the Pleasure Drive
Where everything went by but time; the Study Hour
Spent at a desk, with folded hands, in waiting.

In those I could make. Did I not make in them
Myself? The Grown One whose time shortens,
Breath quickens, heart beats faster, till at last
It catches, skips. . . . Yet those hours that seemed, were endless
Were still not long enough to have remade
My childish heart: the heart that must have, always,
To make anything of anything, not time,
Not time but—
    but, alas! eternity.

[1954]

Birthday

Today being the day, what gift can I give
myself, earth giving none, nor my nearest
relative? I take the gift of coming bombs.
We shall all be dead on a certain day.
I take my last few looks at the surrounding
scene: stone buildings, hard pavements,
noisy streets, trees dying
of carbon dioxide.
May I live to see
this last bomb flower
in the paradise we promised to each other.

The Only Card I Got on My Birthday Was from an Insurance Man

On upland farms into abandoned wells
on a line meridian high
state by state my birthday star comes on
and peers, my birthday night,
and in my eyes it stands while past its light
the world and I turn, just and far, till
every well scans over the year like spokes
of a wheel returning the long soft look of the sky.

Star in a well, dark message: when I die,
my glance drawn over galaxies,
all through one night let a candle nurse the dark
to mark this instant of what I was,
this once—not putting my hand out
blessing for business' sake any frail markers
of human years: we want real friends or none;
what's genuine will accompany every man.

Who travel these lonely wells can drink that star.

Stefan—A Last Birthday Poem
August 25, 1971

When I pick the wild fig in a hollow
watched over by sand-pines
                    surrounded
by the bright green scrub
shadowing the white sand
                    I bring them in my hat
for you
            in the shade of the scrub-pine where the old
boat waits to be mended
                    Over the red rocks
grow the thorn-trees,
                    pronged
forks splayed
            above the extraordinary
sea
    Odysseus came here & thought
this place enchanted because the green
water has a peacock's tail
We come upon it
suddenly in a hump of this barren
island's coastline
where the sand lies pure on the sky and sea: there
is nothing else here
                Julian Huxley
could have wished to be a heron courting
his mate: rubbing the just-raised
plumes of the other bird again and
again . . ."to such a pitch of emotion
did it bring them"

or like the Crested
Grebe, to dance & dive together
amorously below the water.
Neither of these
celebrations of love is mine,
human I am less
than these,
mortal I dream
of you undying:
that is why
I offer a hatful of wild figs only
to mark the day

IBIZA, 1959

Poem for My Thirty-Ninth Birthday

Itchy with time in the dogday summer stew,
    flesh melting at its creases and salted raw,
I drove the day for breezes. The children blew
    kisses to traffic. In the stubbly jaw
of the bay my wife went wading. In the wood
    a mouse lay torn on stone beside a pool,
an anthill raging in him like a mood
    of the dogday, a weather of the soul.

Waiting by pools for the fish that spins all water
    and the mouse that will come. Steaming on lawns
in a tinkle of gin. Spraying my birdy daughter,
    my guppy-bubbling son, and nodding like bones
on the leash of love, I heard the wind go over
    like jet-scream, the fact gone before the sound
ripped at the world. And naked as a lover
    I watched a pointed moon sprout from the ground.

It was too thin to die to. Fat as meat,
    I stood alive into my thirty-ninth year
from the deaddog day of summer, the shag heat
    still matted like wet wool on the midnight air,
and took my death for reason. Here it was
    the red worm pushed a nerve-end onto rock.
The world began with women in the house,
    and men with wine jugs waiting on the walk.

Over and through the reefs the thin moon skids,
    the great squid of the storm squirts down the air.
A clam of light glints out of swollen lids.

Flying fish leap at the barrier.
There goes the moon, shipwrecked on churning stone.
What holds the weather up? A raging Morse
flickers along the reef. Let down! Let down!
But the moon rides up and holds, dead to its curse.

A specimen ego pokes into the hour—
news from the sea my mother's screaming broke.
I ate her in her pain. Manchild and sour
from the sea's gland, I sweetened as I woke
out of her milk. But if the land was love,
it was half-terror and too big to dare.
In a great plain, the ticking grass above
my head and reach, I waited with my ear

to the thudding ground. What passed me out of sight?
My father was one. When I had died enough
I made a perfect pink boy of my fright
and used him to forgive time and myself.
Thirty-nine dying birthday years behind,
he listens at the children's sleep and goes
sighing with love and pity to the blind
and breathing love's-bed at the long thought's close.

Here in the thought, outside my house in time,
the year comes where it is. I watch it down
under a moon rubbed like a garlic spline
to a last skin. The river, thick as stone
sweats beads out of the air. A waiting man,
itchy with time and damp as I was born,
I count my birthdays grave by grave, and stand
watching the weather tremble to the storm

that cooked all day while I strolled death by death
by pools, by lawns, by sea, and all my loves.
Time as it is. A laboring to breath
in the clogged air. A nudging at what shoves.

A tapping at what blows. A waiting still
        at the sweet fear and bittering appetite.
A ghost that will not and a ghost that will
        burn faster as it burns out of the night

where all men are their fathers and their sons
        in a haunted house of mirrors to the end.
I have walked my deaths out of a day of bones
        and put my loves to bed, and free, and found
in the labouring summer flesh of man, I wait
        easy enough for the lit nerve and hover
of thunderheads to bolt the moon and break
        the stuck air open, like a death blown over.

Middle Age

Now the midwinter grind
is on me, New York
drills through my nerves,
as I walk
the chewed-up streets.

At forty-five,
what next, what next?
At every corner,
I meet my Father,
my age, still alive.

Father, forgive me
my injuries,
as I forgive
those I
have injured!

You never climbed
Mount Sion, yet left
dinosaur
death-steps on the crust,
where I must walk.

Birthday Poem

When the Hellgate wind unwinds down the canyon
and I wade in my tallest boots
one drift at a time; when that white devil
spins back mean in my teeth, the whole
jaw aching, I sometimes enter
the largest pyramid of all
and fail to emerge from the other side.

Some days that soft intruder climbs the window
ledge I watch, snowbound
at home. His face lights a clear moment, goes out
in chaff. My pulse slows down,
guides the writing hand. I sit with the lights off
tracing hard angles on the pane, sheer fall and rise
of the brain's oscillograph.

Carnations arrive
from Wylie Street where danger's kept
insured. Blear wash of sun
in broken ground. I follow engraved wheels to food,
one tread at a time. A Pinto clanking chains
recalls the heavy end of a car,
nose down in the ditch. Pale weeds by the road
mime themselves before going out unwept.

By midnight, the engine overhauled, shipshape. Cold
settles down beside me when I crawl
between the sheets. Flowers in their own dark
flash under lids: white pink, white yellow,
white-violet-red. All of us drink deep that life-
replenishing powder. I sleep in my shroud sail
like a first-class martyr.

Gift for My Mother's 90th Birthday

We watched the rain sluice down
against the window of your sterile room
and listened as you told of childhood's
summer showers at the farm; how you ran out
a colt unpenned, into their sudden soaking bliss.

Now you, aged changeling mother,
emptied and clean as a cracked china cup
on the wrong shelf, whisper, "What I would give
to feel that rain pelt hard against my face."

But you had nothing left, so we
conspirators of love, locked the white door
and your granddaughter wheeled you to the bath
where we unclothed your little sack of bones
and lifted you beneath the shower.

She held you up, your legs pale stalks a-dangle
and clasped your wasted body, bracing her taut
young flesh to your slack folds.
And you clung laughing, joyous as a child
to feel the clear fresh rivulets
course down your upturned face.

[1991]

Birthday Card for a Psychiatrist

Your friends come fondly to your living room
believing, my dear, that the occasion's mild.
Who still feels forty as a moral *crise*
in this, the Century of the Common Child?

Uncommon gifts, brought to mid-life in pain,
are not a prize. The age demands a cure
for tragedy and gives us brand-new charts
for taking down our psychic temperature.

Othello, of course, regrets having been aggressive,
Hamlet feels pretty silly to think he trusted
terms such as "art" and "honor" instead of "projection,"
and out on the moor King Lear feels maladjusted.

An arrogant richness of the human stuff
is not a value. Nobody wants to be
left holding the bag of himself when all the others
are a democratic homogeneity.

Prospero strips down to his underpants
to teach Miranda that fathers can be informal,
while Cleopatra, Juliet, Rosalind, Kate
fight for the golden apple labelled NORMAL.

In such a state, what laurels can poems bring,
what consolation, what wishes, what advice?
May your conflicts thin out with your hair? BE HAPPY?
We hope you're feeling well? We think you're nice?

Till Burnam Wood shall come to Dunsinane,
till time shall tell us what we really are,
till Responsibility, not Health, defines
the terms of living on this serious star.

The Birthday Dream

At the worst place in the hills above the city
Late at night I was driving cutting through
The overbalancing slums. There was no soul or body
In the streets. I turned right then left somewhere
Near the top, dead-ending into a wall. A car
Pulled out and blocked me. Four men detached from it.
I got out too. It was Saturday night the thrill
Of trouble shimmered on the concrete. One shadow
Had a bottle of wine. I stood and said, say, Buddy,
Give me a drink of that wine not at all fearing
Shaking as on anything but dream bones dream
Feet I would have. He said, We're looking for somebody
To beat up. It won't be me, I said and took him
By the arm with one hand and tossed him into the air.
Snow fell from the clearness in time for there
To be a snowbank for him to fall into elbow-first.
He got up, holding the wine. This guy is too big,
He said, he is too big for us; get the Professor.
Four of us stood together as the wind blew and the snow
Disappeared and watched the lights of the city
Shine some others appearing among them some
Going out and watched the lava-flow of headlights off
In the valley. Like a gunshot in the building next to us
A light went out and down came a middle-aged man
With a hairy chest; his gold-trimmed track shorts had
YMCA Instructor on them and I knew it was time
For the arm game. We stretched out on our stomachs
On top of the dead-end wall. On one side was the drop
We had all been looking into and the other side sank
Away with my car with the men: two darks lifted

Us toward the moon. We put our elbows on the wall
And clasped palms. Something had placed gold-rimmed
Glasses of wine beside us   apartment lights hung in them
Loosely   and we lay nose to nose at the beginning
Of that ceremony; I saw the distant traffic cross him
From eye to eye. Slowly I started to push   and he
To push. My body grew as it lay   forced against his
But nothing moved. I could feel the blood vessels
In my brow distend   extend   grow over the wall like vines
And in my neck   swell like a trumpet player's: I gritted
Into his impassive face   where the far lights moved   this is
What I want   this is what I came for. The city pulsed
And trembled in my arm   shook with my effort   for miles
In ever direction   and from far below in the dark
I heard the voices of men raised up in a cry of wild
Encouragement   of terror   joy   as I strained to push
His locked hand down. I could not move him   did not want
To move him   would not yield. The world strove with my body
To overcome   the highways shuddered   writhed   came apart
At the centerline   far below us a silent train went by
A warning light   and slowly from the embodying air was loaded
With thousands of ghostly new cars   in tiered racks
The lightlike pale wine in their tinted windshields.
The culture swarmed around me like my blood   transfigured
By force. I put my head down and pushed with all my life
And writing sprang under my forehead   onto the concrete:
Graffitti scratched with a nail   a boot heel   an ice pick
A tire iron   a scrap of metal from a stolen car   saying
You are here   and I woke
Entangled with my wife, who labored   pled   screamed
To bring me forth. The room was full of madness. I was forty.

February Twelfth Birthday Statement

That nameless son of a bitch of a critic who
wrote that I only wrote one good poem in
my life might be right so here's to you
future brother and sister and other poets
to drink to me and you with a shot
of bourbon and a bottle of beer
to the success of my intention on
my sixty-fifth birthday and to your
matching accomplishment. One poem
is enough. What have you two done,
my birthday mates Abraham Lincoln
and Tadeusz-Thaddeus Kościuszko,
to get a Lincoln Memorial and a Kos-
iosko Street in Brooklyn? Nothing
but revolutionary activity. That son
of a bitch of a critic has said it: I have
made one poem, not the Gettysburg Address,
and not the military fortifications at West Point.

A Birthday Poem

June 22, 1976

Like a small cloud, like a little hovering ghost
Without substance or edges,
Like a crowd of numbered dots in a sick child's puzzle,
A loose community of midges
Sways in the carven shafts of noon that coast
Down through the summer trees in a golden dazzle.

Intent upon such tiny copter flights,
The eye adjusts its focus
To those billowings about ten feet away,
That hazy, woven hocus-pocus
Or shell game of the air, whose casual sleights
Leave us unable certainly to say

What lies behind it, or what sets it off
With fine diminishings,
Like the pale towns Mantegna chose to place
Beyond the thieves and King of Kings:
Those domes, theatres and temples, clear enough
On that mid-afternoon of our disgrace.

And we know at once it would take an act of will
Plus a firm, inquiring squint
To ignore those drunken motes and concentrate
On the blurred, unfathomed background tint
Of deep sea-green Holbein employed to fill
The space behind his ministers of state,

As if one range slyly obscured the other.
As, in the main, it does.
All of our Flemish distances disclose
A clarity that never was:
Dwarf pilgrims in the green faubourgs of Mother
And Son, stunted cathedrals, shrunken cows.

It's the same with Time. Looked at *sub specie*
Aeternitatis, from
The snow-line of some Ararat of years,
Scholars remark those kingdoms come
To nothing, to grief, without the least display
Of anything so underbred as tears,

And with their Zeiss binoculars decry
Verduns and Waterloos,
The man-made mushroom's deathly overplus,
Caesars and heretics and Jews
Gone down in blood, without batting an eye,
As if all history were deciduous.

It's when we come to shift the gears of tense
That suddenly we note
A curious excitement of the heart
And slight catch in the throat:—
When, for example, from the confluence
That bears all things away I set apart

The inexpressible lineaments of your face,
Both as I know it now,
By heart, by sight, by reverent touch and study,
And as it once was years ago,
Back in some inaccessible time and place,
Fixed in the vanished camera of somebody.

You are four years old here in this photograph.
You are turned out in style,
In a pair of bright red sneakers, a birthday gift.
You are looking down at them with a smile
Of pride and admiration, half
Wonder and half joy, at the right and the left.

The picture is black and white, mere light and shade.
Even the sneakers' red
Has washed away in acids. A voice is spent,
Echoing down the ages in my head:
What is your substance, whereof are you made,
That millions of strange shadows on you tend?

O my most dear, I know the live imprint
Of that smile of gratitude,
Know it more perfectly than any book.
It brims upon the world, a mood
Of love, a mode of gladness without stint.
O that I may be worthy of that look.

Lines on His Birthday

I was born on a street named Joy
of which I remember nothing,
but since I was a boy
I've looked for its lost turning.
Still I seem to hear my mother's cry
echo in the street of joy.
She was sick as Ruth for home
when I was born. My birth
took away my father's wife
and left me half
my life. Christ will my remorse
be less when my father's dead?
Or more. As Lincoln's minister of war
kept the body of his infant boy
in a silver coffin on his desk,
so I keep
in a small heirloom box of teak
the picture of my living father.
Or perhaps it is an image of myself
dead in this box she held?
I know her milk like ivory blood
still runs in my thick veins
and leaves in me an almost
lickerish taste for ghosts:
my mother's wan face,
full brown hair, the mammoth breast
death cuts off at the bone—
to which she draws her bow
again, brazen Amazon,
and aiming deadly as a saint
shoots her barb
of guilt into my game heart.

January 23, 1961

Poem for Your Birthday

This year both our birthdays end in zero,
Symbol, perhaps, of the nothing we'll become
Except as the reflections of our children—
Your boys, my girls,—in the next millenium
Now so near. Who thought we'd see it come?

Let us reflect awhile on us, my dear:
Born fortunate, two creatures petted and well-fed
With milk and vitamins, thus our good teeth and skin;
Curled hair and handmade clothes and patent slippers,
This side of the moat from the desperate unemployed.

Ah yes!—and hasn't that come round again!
We circle back to the fascinating question:
How did we get from there to where we are?
We've perched on the edge of revolution, war,
I, in China, you, in Pakistan.

We both knew children who have died by fire.
We're yoked in sympathy for all that's human,
Having loved those of every tone of skin,
Having lived the loss of extraordinary men.

And the poems we've read aloud to one another!
You wave your arms in a wide arc of rapture,
Moved by the Muse and another glass of wine.
I cherish that characteristic gesture
As you must smile at some oddity of mine.

Truly to relish trivia in flower,
Woman-talk of recipes and clothes,
One must be aware of that high discourse
On art and life we could deal with if we chose.

"The flow of soul," as Pope extravagantly called it,
Unstopped, though years of parting intervene,
Though illness, duties, children interrupt,
We know we'll go on talking till the end

Or after, when we still reach out in thought,
Or waking, sense the living person near.
The password at the boundary is *Friend.*

FOR BARBARA THOMPSON

A Birthday Poem for My Little Sister

Ball of cold metals, shooter of nerve rays, Moon,
Be god yet for poets and their strange loves
Call in the tides of madness that trip us on our way
And help me send a poem of love to my sweet sister
Still darling like when she was a baby
Although now woman-shaped and married.

Dear Barbara, when you had the ear operation
And your hair was cut short like a baby dike
I sat by your crib because I considered you mine
And read you stories of cluck-cluck and moo-moo:
They didn't have to make sense, just noises.

I tried to keep you from masturbating
According to instructions in Parents' Magazine
Which recommended the diversion method rather than threats or
    punishment.
It was no use, your hand preferred your little cunt to toys I offered
Like the ape in the zoo who was jerking off
And all the kids asked their mothers, "What's he doing, ma?"
So the keeper tried to divert him from his hard-on with an ice-cream
cone
But he shifted the cone to the other hand and licked it while he
    went right on.

And then during the war we were both in uniform
You in the Brownies and I in the Air Force:
When I came home that time with silver wings on
You threw yourself into my arms like a furry bundle;
That was your contribution to the war effort, a hug for a soldier

Not bombing the Germans as you were convinced the Brownies
were going to do.
When you were twelve I saw your intellectual possibilities
And took you to a difficult play
Where you fell in love with a faggot actor.
Then I tried modern poetry on you, The Love Song of J. Alfred
Prufrock;
You listened very seriously and remembered the refrain like a
jump-rope poem:
It was odd to hear a little girl reciting those lines.

And suddenly you grew up and went out with boys . . . strangers
And you spoke with them in a language like a code
I mean you became a woman, so I'll never have you again:
There must be a taboo against brothers.
Of course now I have someone of my own who reaches to me
with sweet arms
But the heart is a tree of many seasons
And old loves grow forever deep inside.

The moon rules old loves in their branching
And today the great white magic ball in the sky
Has wound up my heart like on a line of wool
Today on your birthday I remember
How I ran up and down the block knocking on all the doors
To tell the neighbors you were born
(Bored looks, after all you were the sixth child):
I was really announcing that you were born for me and would be mine.

But you grew up and went away and got married
As little girls grow up into women
Leaving us gasping and desperate and hurt.
And we recover and forget, or half-forget
Until sitting down to write a birthday poem we remember everything—
A little girl on her potty hunched seriously to the business
Or holding all of you at once in my arms, colt, calf, and pussy-cat:
All I mean is, I miss you my little sister.

For a Thirteenth Birthday

You have read *War and Peace.*
Now here is *Sister Carrie,*
not up to Tolstoy; still
it will second the real world:
predictable planes and levels,
pavement that holds you,
stairs that lift you,
ice that trips you,
nights that begin after sunset,
four lunar phases,
a finite house.

I give you Dreiser
although (or because)
I am no longer sure.
Lately I have been walking into glass doors.
Through the car windows, curbs disappear.
On the highway, wrong turnoffs become irresistible,
someone else is controlling the wheel.
Sleepless nights pile up like a police record;
all my friends are getting divorced.
Language, my old comrade, deserts me;
words are misused or forgotten,
consonants fight each other
between my upper and lower teeth.
I write *fiend* for *friend*
and *word* for *world,*
remember comes out with an *m* missing.

* * *

I used to be able to find my way in the dark,
sure of the furniture,
but the town I lived in for years
has pulled up its streets in my absence,
disguised its buildings behind my back.
My neighbor at dinner glances
at his cuffs, his palms;
he has memorized certain phrases,
no one at the table does.

And so I give you Dreiser,
his measure of certainty:
a table that's oak all the way through,
real and fragrant flowers,
skirts from sheep and silkworms,
no unknown fibers;
a language as plain as money,
a workable means of exchange;
a world whose very meanness is solid,
mud into mortar, and you are sure
of what will injure you.

I give you names like nails,
walls that withstand your pounding,
doors that are hard to open,
but once they are open, admit you
into rooms that breathe pure sun.
I give you trees that lose their leaves,
as you knew they would,
and then come green again.
I give you
fruit preceded by flowers,
Venus supreme in the sky,
the miracle of always
landing on your feet,
even though the earth
rotates on its axis.

Start out with that, at least.

I have stopped being the heroine
of my bad dreams. The melodramas
of betrayal and narrow escapes
from which I wake up grateful
for an unexciting life
are starring my troubled young friend
or one of my daughters. I'm not the one
who swims too far out to sea;
I am the one who waves from shore
vainly and in despair.
Life is what happens to someone else;
I stand on the sidelines and wring my hands.
Strange that my dreams should have accepted
the minor role I've been cast in
by stories since stories began.
Does that mean I have solved my life?
I'm still afraid in my dreams, but not for myself.
Fear gets rededicated
with a new stone that bears a needier name.

On Approaching My Birthday

My mother bore me in the heat of summer
when the grass blanched under sun's hammer stroke
and the birds sang off key, panting between notes,
and the pear trees once all winged with whiteness
sagged, breaking with fruit, and only the zinnias,
like harlots, bloomed out vulgar and audacious,
and when the cicadas played all day long
their hidden harpsichords accompanying
her grief, my mother bore me, as I say,
then died shortly thereafter, no doubt
of her disgust and left me her disease
when I grew up to wither into truth.

Birthday

It is that they spend so much time in the sky
that bluebirds have streaks of red across their chests;
and it is that—except for the robbing of their houses—
they came north for my birthday bringing the light
of southern Texas with them. Every year
I am able to do the mathematics
and stand like another bird—outside my door—
with one foot in and one foot out, half-looking
for the first light and whisper one phrase or other—
one or the other—and look for a streak of red
and a flash of blue. If you asked me what I lived for
I'd say it was for knowledge; I'd never say
I was waiting to see the sun come up
behind the willow; or I'd say I was living to see
the bluebirds come east again; I'd never say
I was waiting for justice, or I was waiting
for vengeance and recovery; I'd say
I was waiting to see the thumbnail moon
at five o'clock in the evening, or I was waiting
to see what shape it takes by morning or when
it becomes an acorn moon. I'd never say
the bluebird has disappeared from the east, the starling
has driven him out; I'd never turn to the starling
and the English sparrow and hate them for their stubbornness—
how could I as a Jew?—I'd never say
the pigeon is our greatest pest; how could I
who came from New York City myself? I'd say
it's too late to go to Idaho and sight
the distance to the pole; I'd say I'll never
move now to southern Arizona—I'd let

the forest come back to Pennsylvania. I am
half-English when it comes to trees; I live
for the past as much as the future—why should I lie?
I am ruined by the past. I can trace
my eyelids back to central Asia.

It is

when the thaw comes and the birds begin to swell
with confusion and a few wild seeds take hold
and the light explodes a little I lie down
a second time, either to feel the sun
or hear the house shake from the roar of engines
at the end of my street, the train from North Dakota
carrying sweeteners to Illinois, moving
forward a single foot, then backwards another,
one of those dreary mysteries, hours of shrieking
and banging, endless coupling, the perfect noise
to go with my birthday, grief and grinding enough,
wisdom enough, some lily or other growing
on the right-of-way, some brakeman still wearing a suit
from Oshkosh, he and I singing a union song
from 1920, some dead opossum singing
something about a paw-paw tree, his hands
over his eyes, some bluebird greased with corn oil
and dreaming of New York State singing songs
about the ruins or about the exile, notes
from southern Texas, notes from eastern Poland,
drifting into the roundhouse; Lamentations
of 1992, a soft slurring
on her part, a tender rasping on mine,
though both of us loving the smell of mud, I think,
and both of us willing to snap some twigs, although for different rea-
sons I think, and both of us loving
light above all else, almost a craving
that occupied our minds in late February
and made us forget the darkness and the wobbling
between two worlds that overwhelmed us only
a month or two before. It has to be
the oldest craving of all, the first mercy.

Poem for My 20th Birthday

Passing the American graveyard, for my birthday
the crosses stuttering, white on tropical green,
the year's quick focus of faces I do not remember. . .

The palm trees, stalking the deliberate giants
for my birthday, and all the hot adolescent memories
seen through a screen of water.

For my birthday thrust into the adult and actual:
expected to perform the action, not to ponder
the reality beyond the fact,
the man standing upright in the dream.

A Birthday Candle

Thirty today, I saw
The trees flare briefly like
The candles on a cake,
As the sun went down the sky,
A momentary flash,
Yet there was time to wish

Before the light could die,
If I had known what to wish,
As once I must have known,
Bending above the clean
Candlelit tablecloth
To blow them out with a breath.

Poem on My Birthday

In Canada, on a dark afternoon,
from a cabin beside Lake Purgatory
I saw your two clenched fists in a tree
—your most recent rage, until I came to my senses,
and saw two small lighted glass lamps reflected
through a window onto the maple leaves.
Was it simply that I had stolen away
in the wilderness to go fishing on my birthday,
twelve years after your death, and you
less than your rusty pliers in my fishing box?

It is late August in the moral North.
To answer your first question
—I obey the fish and game laws
of New York State, Ontario, and Quebec.
The odd branch has already turned red,
as for me I have turned inside out,
I cry for revolution against myself
—no longer red, I'm parlor pink and grey,
you, less than a thumb print on a page.

Matters still outstanding: you will not remember
a boy, I cut school, sneak out
to the 42nd street library to read among readers
like a stray lion cub taken into a great pride.
I have kept your Greek grammar,
your 78 revolutions per minute
recording of Rossini's *Barber*
you played to stop me from crying,
almost my first memory.

Your *valuable papers,* now valuable
only to me, I fed to a fire years ago.
Frankly I am tired of receiving letters from the dead
every day, and carrying you on my back,
out of the burning city,
in and out of the bathroom and bedroom,
you less than the smoke you wanted for a shroud.

Let us dance with Sarah behind the curtain
where God in his divine humor
tells Abraham Sarah will at 90 bear a son,
and she asks laughing within herself, "Will I have pleasure?"
Take one foot, then the other . . . Imitate a departure
if you make it not, and each going
will lend a kind of easiness to the next.
Father, you poisoned my father.
I am standing alone, telling the truth
as you commanded. (Without too many
of the unseemly details, like the sounds of you in bed
sucking, I thought, on fruit, I later would not eat.)
You, less than a seed of a wild grape.

Today, in the last moments of light
I heard a fish, a "Musky", your nickname, break water.
As I sing my song of how you
will be remembered, if I could
out of misericordia, I'd tie you to the mast
and stuff your ears with wax. I regret
some parts of the body forgive, some don't. Father,
do not forget your 18 inch Board of Education ruler
on which I measured my penis, marking its progress,
you kept on your desk before you till your old age
—one reason, perhaps, for the archaic Greek smile
I wore on my face through boyhood.
I never thought I'd dig your grave with laughter.

PHILIP BOOTH

Sixty-six

Waking himself,
without any alarm,
after an after-
lunch nap not a half-
hour before the
burial service, he
reached for the
motel note-pad beside
the head of his
bed to find the six
words, the six
profound words he was
sure, getting
up for this afternoon's
interment, he
had, going to sleep,
written down.
The words had made beautiful
sense, sense he
now sensed as terrible
loss, now that
both he and the words were
beyond whatever
it was they meant when
they came to him
from wherever they'd come.
And had now
gone back to; or altogether
gone out of the
world in having gone out

of his head. No,
that wasn't true. Buttoning up
his blue button-
down, hoisting his pants, tying
his tie in the
mirror, and combing, he knew that
those words, all
six, though far from him and
each other, were,
in one form or another, surely
at home in his
old Unabridged. From which, in
due time, if he
refound two, and could, for the life
of him, keep his
mind open, all might come back.
Rechecking his
fly, he straightened up, checked
again how he
looked, took his flightbag out to
the car, backed
to drop off on the TV top
his key to the
wordless motel, and drove
to the graveside.

On My Birthday

I swam in the sea our mother
Naked as the day I was born
Still fit at forty-four
Willing to live forever

49th Birthday Trip (What Are You On?)

I close my eyes
Avoid the rush
Sometimes I doze
Inside the bus
If I arrive
At six-fifteen
Will I be seen?
Seven times seven
Makes forty-nine
Even at eleven
I was on time

Five Words for Joe Dunn on His 22nd Birthday

I shall give you five words for your birthday.

The first is *anthropos*
Who celebrates birthdays.
He is withered and tough and blind, babbler
Of old wars and dead beauty.
He is there for the calmness of your heart as the days race
And the wars are lost and the roses wither.
No enemy can strike you that he has not defeated.
No beauty can die in your heart that he will not remember.

The second word is *andros*
Who is proud of his gender,
Wears it like a gamecock, erects it
Through the midnight of time
Like a birthday candle.
He will give you wisdom like a Fool
Hidden in the loins
Crying out against the inelegance
Of all that is not sacred.

The third word is *eros*
Who will cling to you every birthnight
Bringing your heart substance.
Whomever you touch will love you,
Will feel the cling of His touch upon you
Like sunlight scattered over an ancient mirror.

The fourth word is *thanatos,* the black belly
That eats birthdays
I do not give you *thanatos.* I bring you a word to call Him
Thanatos, devourer of young men, heart-biter, bone-licker.
Look, He slinks away when you name Him.
Name Him! *Thanatos.*

The last word is *agape*,
The dancer that puts birthdays in motion.
She is there to lead words.
Counter to everything. She makes words
Circle around Her. Words dance.
See them. *Anthropos* ageless.
Andros made virgin, *Eros* unmirrored
Thanatos devoured.
Agape, *Agape*, ring-mistress,
Love
That comes from beyond birthdays,
That makes poetry
And moves stars.

Birthday Poem

I am born at home
the last of four children.
The doctor brings me as promised
in his snap-jawed black leather satchel.

He takes me out in sections
fastens limbs to torso
torso to neck stem
pries Mama's navel open
and inserts me, head first.

Chin back, I swim upward
up the alimentary canal
bypassing mouth and nose holes
and knock at the top
of her head to be let out
wherefore her little bald spot.

Today my mother is eighty-two
splendidly braceleted and wigged.
She had to go four times to the well
to get me.

A Birthday

Shall we address it
as you, lovely one,
singing those intervals

of a complex
loneliness, a wanting too
to know

its condition. Together
is one by one,
and a beauty

comes of it, a substance
of beauty—beauty, *beauty*—
dripping its condition.

I had thought
a moment of stasis
possible, some

thing fixed—
days, worlds—
but what I know

is water, as you
are water, as you
taught me water

is wet. Now slowly
spaces occur, a ground is
disclosed as dirt. The

mountains come of it,
the sky precedes, and where
there had been only

land now sticks and stones
are evident. So we are
here, so we are.

Birthday Poem to My Wife

Have you considered how inconsequential we all
are: I mean, in the long term: but

anything getting closer to now—deaths, births,
marriages, murders—grows the consequence

till if you kissed me that would be a matter
of great consequence: large spaces also include

us into anonymity, but you beside me, as the
proximity heightens, declares myself, and you, to

the stars: not a galaxy refuses its part in
spelling our names: thus you understand if you

go out in the back yard or downtown to the
grocery store—or take a plane to Paris—

time pours in around me and space
devours me and like inconsequence I'm little and lost.

John Button Birthday

Sentiments are nice, "The Lonely Crowd,"
a rift in the clouds appears above the purple,
you find a birthday greeting card with violets
which says "a perfect friend" and means
"I love you" but the customer is forced to be
shy. It says less, as all things must.

But
grease sticks to the red ribs shaped like a
sea shell, grease, light and rosy that smells of
saldalwood: it's memory! I remember JA
staggering over to me in the San Remo and murmuring
"I've met someone MARVELLOUS!" That's friendship
for you, and the sentiment of introduction.

And now that I have finished dinner I can continue.

What is it that attracts one to one? Mystery?
I think of you in Paris with a red beard, a
theological student; in London talking to a friend
who lunched with Dowager Queen Mary and offered
her his last cigarette; in Los Angeles shopping
at the Supermarket; on Mount Shasta, looking . . .
above all on Mount Shasta in your unknown youth
and photograph.

And then the way you straighten
people out. How ambitious you are! And that you're
a painter is a great satisfaction, too. You know how

I feel about painters. I sometimes think poetry
only describes.

Now I have taken down the underwear
I washed last night from the various light fixtures
and can proceed.

And the lift of our experiences
together, which seem to me legendary. The long subways
to our old neighborhood the near East 49th and 53rd,
and before them the laughing in bars till we cried,
and the crying in movies till we laughed, the tenting
tonight on the old camp grounds! How beautiful it is
to visit someone for instant coffee and you visiting
Cambridge, Massachusetts, talking for two weeks worth
in hours, and watching Maria Tallchief in the Public
Gardens while the swan-boats slumbered. And now,
not that I'm interrupting again, I mean your now,
you are 82 and I am 03. And in 1984 I trust we'll still
be high together. I'll say "Let's go to a bar"
and you'll say "Let's go to a movie" and we'll go to both;
like two old Chinese drunkards arguing about their
favorite mountain and the million reasons for them both.

To Canada (For Washington's Birthday)

I shall be so glad when you come down
like a Grand Polonaise out of the ice and strangeness
bringing me out of the strangeness and ice
I am so tired of the limitations of immobility
all of America pretending to be a statue
or an African mask making up cigar-rituals
who gives a damn if we ordered enough cigars from Cuba
before we broke off relations (though we did)
and used them to light those fires in Harlem doorways
(everyone knows who that arsonist is) I am
so sick of the pretensions of their worried faces
that worried look too is a valiant attempt to be blind
and I am so weary of their sexual importance
consisting chiefly in "not being had" oh Poles
I'd rather be leaping off the brink of a precipice
with you or eating terrible herring in Toronto
or merluza in Barcelona that tastes like a sandal
I don't care how dark it gets as long as we can still move!
I can't sit here listening to Chopin for the rest of my life!
oh what's the use I think I will

On A Birthday of Kenneth's

Kenny!
Kennebunkport! I see you standing there
assuaging everything with your smile
at the end of the world you are scratching your head wondering what is
that funny French word Roussel was so fond of? oh "dénouement"!
and it is good

I knew prefectly well that afternoon on the grass when you read Vincent
and me your libretto that you had shot out of the brassière factory
straight into the blue way ahead of the Russians (what do they know
now that Pasternak is gone) and were swinging there like a Strad
And that other day when we heard Robert Frost read your poems for
the Library of Congress we admired you too though we didn't like the
way he read "Mending Sump"
and when Mrs. Kennedy bought your drawing that was a wonderful day
too

but in a sense these days didn't add up to a year
and you haven't had a birthday
you have simply the joyous line of your life like in a Miró

no wonder I felt so lonely on Saturday when you didn't give your annual
cocktail party!
I didn't know why

Ode: My 24th Year

Now I have become a man
and know no more than mankind can
and groan with nature's every grown,
transcending child's blind skeleton
and all childish divinity,
while loomed in consanguinity
the weaving of the shroud goes on.

No two things alike; and yet
first memory dies, then I forget
one carnal thought that made thought grim:
but that has sunk below time's rim
and wonder ageing into woe
later dayes more fatal show:
Time gets thicker, light gets dim.

And I a second Time am blind,
all starlight dimmed out of the mind
that was first candle to the morn,
and candelabra turned to thorn.
All is dream till morn has rayed
the Rose of night back into shade,
Messiah firmament reborn.

Now I cannot go be wild
or harken back to shape of child.
chrystal born into the aire
circled by the harte and bear
and agelesse in a greene arcade,
for he is down in Granite laid,
or standing on a Granite stair.

No return, where thought's completed;
let that ghost's last gaze go cheated:
I may waste my days no more
pining in spirituall warre.
Where am I in wilderness?
What creature bore my bones to this?
Here is no Eden: this is my store.

September 1950–1951

Lighting Your Birthday Cake

Of course we didn't come this far
without leaving a trail, but it's only
footprints on a beach: one wash
through our memories, and it's gone. Strange,
so much passion, commitment, doomed
to be drifted over like
Troy and Babylon, pitiful echoes now
of all those eager heartbeats.
You've always cared so much,
about us, sure, but really everything—
hungry kids, dolphins, over-
population, and the old foes: batterers, bishops,
gunslingers, chauvinists—nothing escapes
your rage or compassion; earthquakes in Asia
shake our midnight bedroom. You always knew
that the bright bird of sympathy
is the only godliness on earth,
hovering over these grubby streets
on better wings than angels'. Now
I can't believe in a world without
your bonfire of outrage, small flame of anguish,
pink glow of happiness.
Remember how I need your warmth:
as you blow out these candles, make a wish
to keep the fires burning.

In the Winter of My Thirty-Eighth Year

It sounds unconvincing to say *When I was young*
Though I have long wondered what it would be like
To be me now
No older at all it seems from here
As far from myself as ever

Waking in fog and rain and seeing nothing
I imagine all the clocks have died in the night
Now no one is looking I could choose my age
It would be younger I suppose so I am older
It is there at hand I could take it
Except for the things I think I would do differently
They keep coming between they are what I am
They have taught me little I did not know when I was young

There is nothing wrong with my age now probably
It is how I have come to it
Like a thing I kept putting off as I did my youth

There is nothing the matter with speech
Just because it lent itself
To my uses

Of course there is nothing the matter with the stars
It is my emptiness among them
While they drift farther away in the invisible morning

First Day Of The Future

They always seem to come up
on the future, these cold, earthly dawns;
the whiteness and the blackness
make the flesh shiver as though it's starting to break.
But that is always just an illusion,
always it is just another day they illuminate
of the permanent present. Except for today.
A motorboat sets out across the bay,
a transfiguring spirit, all its little puffy gasps
of disintegration collected
and anthemed out in a pure purr of dominion.
It disappears. In the stillness again
the shore lights remember the dimensions of the black water.
I don't know about this new life.
Even though I burned the ashes of its flag again and again
and set fire to the ticket that might have conscripted me into its ranks
        forever,
even though I squandered all my talents composing my emigration
        papers,
I think I want to go back now and live again in the present time, back there
where someone milks a cow and jets of intensest nourishment go
        squawking into a pail,
where someone is hammering, a bit of steel at the end of a stick hitting
        a bit of steel, in the archaic stillness of an afternoon,
or somebody else saws a board, back and forth, like hard labor
in the lungs of one who refuses to come to the very end.
But I guess I'm here. So I must take care. For here
one has to keep facing the right way, or one sees one dies, and one dies.
I'm not sure I'm going to like it living here in the future.
I don't think I can keep on doing it indefinitely.

At Sixty

I have pried up, brushed off the self in me
that hugged secrets—the griever, the night walker,
the peeping-tom who promised to reform,
thumbing through porn all day. Acknowledge all
his lapses, his intensity. Never fault him for feeling:
fault him for what he endangered: creeping into
beds so sweet that he could not recall the breathing.
He bubbled promises to keep his lovers
deaf to the lofty inflections of a desire
that had no mind to remember what it had sworn,
or whom it had been sworn to, or when. Could he expect
to anticipate the lurches of his guilt?

Well, things have changed for the good. The world looks clear.
That self has bleached: his harshest needs are gone.
Yet sometimes at the drawing in of day
when I am too beaten down to lift a spoon
I taste the sharp pepper of his cruelty.

Safety at Forty: or, an Abecedarian Takes a Walk

Alfa is nice. Her Roman eye
Is outlined in an O of dark
Experience. She's thirty-nine.
Would it not be kind of fine
To take her quite aback, affront
Her forward manner, take her up
On it? Echo: of course it would.

Betta is nice. Her Aquiline
Nose prowly marches out between
Two raven wings of black sateen
Just touched, at thirty-five, with gray.
What if I riled her quiet mien
With an indecent, subterrene
Proposal? She might like me to.

Gemma is nice. Her Modenese
Zagato body, sprung on knees
As supple as steel coils, shocks
Me into plotting to acquire
The keys to her. She's twenty-nine.
Might I aspire to such a fine
Consort in middle age? Could be.

Della is nice. Calabrian
Suns engineered the sultry tan
Over (I'm guessing) all of her long
And filly frame. She's twenty-one.
Should I consider that she might

Look kindly on my graying hairs
And my too-youthful suit? Why not?

O Megan, all-American
Wife waiting by the hearth at home,
As handsome still at forty-five
As any temptress now alive,
Must I confess my weariness
At facing stringent mistresses
And head for haven? Here I come.

Kaherawak's Birthday—July 28
My First Granddaughter

Crow caws against grey skies,
flies nibble the elbow as a breeze
off the summer river lifts hair
from my face waiting for sun after rain.
Letters to friends are waiting, sealed,
for posting as black-eyed susans and golden-rod
sway in down-fields bursting blooms
as dried raspberry pellets thump earth
from brambles that have completed
the labor of centuries. Noon slowly
approaches with the whistle of a train
riding the rails across the river in Canada,
disturbs the tabby cat's sleep under another
screech of crow flapping wings high
over the island. Movement by stealth movement like spider
sun at last emerges in the southern sphere.
Things splash yellow . . . even green leaves
of sumac and poplar are tainted, brushed.
Finch sings a warning to starling,
swallow zooms through the air expecting insects;
the currant is bare, the berries eaten by goats;
corn is dry but beans are heavy and onions
ready for pulling.

This is your birthday gift . . .
this summer day and all its riches: snores
of the dog, heal-all, purple burdock,
thistle; winds and birds, weasel in the grass,
mice in the barn, berries jammed for winter, spiders,
grandma's smile, sun; turtle slipping from mud;
bear reaching into gnarled trees for honey; wolf

roaming the distant Adirondacks
and Grandmother Moon waning now in late July,
commanding her strength
to rise again tonight to bathe the dark
in colors of harvest orange which will tip
bat wings, stars and clouds drifting,
and move the river to the sea,
illuminate western wind, bring good dreams
to your sleep, happy days to your
accumulating years on this earth, years
in which you will learn to thank the sun,
Grandmother Moon, the corn and beans and squash,
the berries, herbs, the useful birds and dragon-flies,
bees, the elm and maple that reach at night
to stars that guide the hunger in the woods, light
the fisherman's path and glisten
on the scales of the fish themselves.
You will learn to thank the mysteries,
movements above and below the earth,
below the four winds, the four colors,
the four directions.

Tonight

your father will play his guitar and sing a song
and then have a good, long smoke
while crow sleeps in its nest away from your dreams
under the lingering scent of strawberry leaves.

This is your birthday gift . . .
the old stories of the sky, waters, the earth
and winds. One day when old you, too,
will tell them on into time within the sounds
of the drum, the quiet of the mountain, the silent flow of the river.
Yes, good dreams,
good journey, many moons,
and sweet winds for your pillow.

Cornwall Island
Akwesasne 1983

For Helene On Her 30th Birthday

The runt of the litter
of seven little girls.

I don't want to spend
too much time on the idea
of how deprived you were.
There is already too much
pity in this world,
nor get saccharine about you
rocking me to sleep in your arms
and baking bread in a hot oven,
or breaking your back
in a field of blueberries.
Nor remind you of how you favored
my sister, or denied me for the man
whose puke you've cleaned up for years.
I've pretty much forgotten that.
However, I doubt we ever forgive.
There's enough distance now
to separate fact from fiction
and to remind myself
you were/are a woman . . .
capable of being human . . .
your skin wrinkles as does mine,
your flesh withers.
We're of the same cut;
the same cotton cloth.
I knew your wet nipples;
you knew my sharp teething.
Mama, they called

very late the other night
Woke me up at 3 a.m.
What could I say at such an hour,
what could I do.
I couldn't rock you in my arms,
nor stuff you into a tote bag
and ride Greyhound to California
where you'd be safe in the sun.
Nor could I convince them
that a woman is not a Ford,
that when it stops running
you take it to the junkyard
and sell it for used parts.
They wouldn't buy that.

Mama we're all runts.

Eventually we'll all
be placed away from ourselves
where we can't harm
ourselves; where the tough
and strong won't need to worry
nor interrupt the baseball game
to check if we're all right
lighting the kitchen stove.

Mama, shake your head.
Bite the first hand that puts
a finger on your arm.

Writ on the Eve of My 32nd Birthday
a slow thoughtful spontaneous poem

I am 32 years old
and finally I look my age, if not more.
Is it a good face what's no more a boy's face?
It seems fatter. And my hair,
it's stopped being curly. Is my nose big?
The lips are the same.
And the eyes, ah the eyes get better all the time.
32 and no wife, no baby; no baby hurts,
        but there's lots of time.
I don't act silly any more.
And because of it I have to hear from so-called friends:
"You've changed. You used to be so crazy so great."
They are not comfortable with me when I'm serious.
Let them go to the Radio City Music Hall.
32; saw all of Europe, met millions of people;
        was great for some, terrible for others.
I remember my 31st year when I cried:
"To think I may have to go another 31 years!"
I don't feel that way this birthday.
I feel I want to be wise with white hair in a tall library
        in a deep chair by a fireplace.
Another year in which I stole nothing.
8 years now and haven't stole a thing!
I stopped stealing.
But I still lie at times,
and still am shameless yet ashamed when it comes
        to asking for money.
32 years old and four hard real funny sad bad wonderful
        books of poetry

—the world owes me a million dollars.
I think I had a pretty weird 32 years.
And it weren't up to me, none of it.
No choice of two roads; if there were,
        I don't doubt I'd have chosen both.
I like to think *chance* had it I play the bell.
The clue, perhaps, is in my unabashed declaration:
"I'm good example there's such a thing as called soul."
I love poetry because it makes me love
        and presents me life.
And of all the fires that die in me,
there's one burns like the sun;
it might not make day my personal life,
        my association with people,
        or my behavior toward society,
but it does tell me my soul has a shadow.

I am 25

With a love a madness for Shelly
Chatterton Rimbaud
and the needy-yap of my youth
          has gone from ear to ear:
     I HATE OLD POETMEN!
Especially old poetmen who retract
who consult other old poetmen
who speak their youth in whispers,
saying:—I did those when
          but that was then
          that was then—
O I would quiet old men
say to them:—I am your friend
               what you once were, thru me
               you'll be again—
Then at night in the confidence of their homes
rip out their apology-tongues
               and steal their poems.

For Lucy, *On Her Birthday*

Were you born as I was, beautiful witch?

I think you were spun by spiders
on a black mountain.

How woman were you I took as only woman
then there was magic, and before I knew
you were wind and dust and summer days
rain across the window
cold and holy water

and white fire.

What can I bring, extraordinary woman?
Wings of bats

or moon dark?

Birthday Poem

The sun rose today, and
The sun went down
Over the trees beyond the river;
No crashing thunder
Nor jagged lightning
Flashed my fourty-four years across
The heavens. I am here.
I am alone. With the Indianapolis / News

Sitting, under this indiana sky
I lean against a gravestone and feel
The warm wine on my tongue.
My eyes move along the corridors
Of the stars, searching
For a sign, for a certainty

As definite as the cold concrete
Pressing against my back.
Still the stars mock
Me and the moon is my judge.

But only the moon.

'Cause I ain't screwed no thumbs
Nor dropped no bombs—
Tho my name is naughty to the ears of some

As / my / belly / becomes a drum and my blood beseech thee—
As / my / heart / becomes a song and my eyes lakes of lightning.

As / your / mother grunts for 3 / days and groans for 3 / nights,
As / she issues you / forth on a sunday night,
                    (on a chilling, raining, sun / day / night)—
                    and now.
As you lay warming in my arms, son—
                    all I / can / say is:
You / be a loonngg time coming, boy—
But you're wel / come here.

November–December 1978

A Poem for a Certain Lady on Her 33rd Birthday

Who are we
to ride the curves of air
or to worry about the waning moon?
The mountains will not tremble
and the sea will not give up her dead.

Time is now, said the African Poet.
Unfelt as our touch
across these seasons
unending as the circle
of our dead fathers and unborn sons—
the rise and fall of our laughter—
the measure of our steps
as we move
to each other.

Years are strips of tinsel
hanging on hunky brains
Our time is the constant blooming
of our love.

A Birthday Present

What is this, behind this veil, is it ugly, is it beautiful?
It is shimmering, has it breasts, has it edges?

I am sure it is unique, I am sure it is just what I want.
When I am quiet at my cooking I feel it looking, I feel it thinking

"Is this the one I am to appear for,
Is this the elect one, the one with black eye-pits and a scar?

Measuring the flour, cutting off the surplus,
Adhering to rules, to rules, to rules.

Is this the one for the annunciation?
My god, what a laugh!"

But it shimmers, it does not stop, and I think it wants me.
I would not mind if it was bones, or a pearl button.

I do not want much of a present, anyway, this year.
After all I am alive only by accident.

I would have killed myself gladly that time any possible way.
Now there are these veils, shimmering like curtains,

The diaphanous satins of a January window
White as babies' bedding and glittering with dead breath. O ivory!

It must be a tusk there, a ghost-column.
Can you not see I do not mind what it is?

Can you not give it to me?
Do not be ashamed—I do not mind if it is small.

Do not be mean, I am ready for enormity.
Let us sit down to it, one on either side, admiring the gleam,

The glaze, the mirrory variety of it.
Let us eat our last supper at it, like a hospital plate.

I know why you will not give it to me,
You are terrified

The world will go up in a shriek, and your head with it,
Bossed, brazen, an antique shield,

A marvel to your great-grandchildren.
Do not be afraid, it is not so.

I will only take it and go aside quietly.
You will not even hear me opening it, no paper crackle,

No falling ribbons, no scream at the end.
I do not think you credit me with this discretion.

If you only knew how the veils were killing my days.
To you they are only transparencies, clear air.

But my god, the clouds are like cotton.
Armies of them. They are carbon monoxide.

Sweetly, sweetly I breathe in,
Filling my veins with invisibles, with the million

Probable motes that tick the years off my life.
You are silver-suited for the occasion. O adding machine——

* * *

Is it impossible for you to let something go and have it go whole?
Must you stamp each piece in purple,

Must you kill what you can?
There is this one thing I want today, and only you can give it to me.

It stands at my window, big as the sky.
It breathes from my sheets, the cold dead centre

Where spilt lives congeal and stiffen to history.
Let it not come by the mail, finger by finger.

Let it not come by word of mouth, I should be sixty
By the time the whole of it was delivered, and too numb to use it.

Only let down the veil, the veil, the veil.
If it were death

I would admire the deep gravity of it, its timeless eyes.
I would know you were serious.

There would be a nobility then, there would be a birthday.
And the knife not carve, but enter

Pure and clean as the cry of a baby,
And the universe slide from my side.

Upon the Last Day of His Forty-Ninth Year

Scritch, scratch, saith the frozen spring snow—
not near enough this season or the last,
but still a skin for skiing on, with care.
At every shaky turn into the fall line
one hundred eighty pounds of tired blood
and innards weakly laced with muscle seek
to give themselves to gravity and ruin.
My knees, a-tremble with old reflex, resist

and try to find the lazy dancer's step
and pillowed curve my edges flirted with
when I had little children to amaze
and life seemed endlessly flexible. Now,
my heavy body swings to face the valley
and feels the gut pull of steep maturity.

A Birthday Memorial To Seventh Street

I

I tarry in days shaped like the high staired street
where I became a woman
between two funeral parlors next door to each other
sharing a dwarf
who kept watch for the hearses
Fox's Bar on the corner
playing happy birthday to a boogie beat
Old slavic men cough in the spring thaw
hawking
painted candles cupcakes fresh eggs
from under their dull green knitted caps
when the right winds blow
the smell of bird seed and malt
from the breweries across the river
stops even our worst hungers.

One crosstown bus each year
carries silence into overcrowded hallways
plucking madmen out of the mailboxes
from under stairwells
from cavorting over rooftops in the full moon
cutting short the mournful songs that used to soothe me
before they would cascade to laughter every afternoon
at four PM
behind a door that never opened
Then masked men in white coats dismount

to take the names of anyone
who has not paid the rent in three months
they peel off layers of christmas seals
and batter down the doors into bare apartments
where they duly note the shape of each obscenity
upon the wall
and hunt those tenants down
to make new vacancies.

II

These were some of my lovers who were processed
through the corridors of Bellevue Mattewean Brooklyn State
the Women's House of D. St. Vincent's and the Tombs
to be stapled on tickets for a one way ride
on the unmarked train that travels
once a year
across the country east to west
filled with New York's rejected lovers
ones who played with all their stakes
who could not win nor learn to lie—
we were much fewer then—
who failed the entry tasks of Seventh Street
and were returned back home
to towns with names like Oblong and Vienna
(called Vyanna)
Cairo Sesser Cave-In-Rock and Legend.
Once a year the train stops unannounced
at midnight
just outside of town
returning the brave of Bonegap and Tuskegee
of Pawnee Falls and Rabbittown
of Anazine and Elegant and Intercourse
leaving them beyond the edge of town
like dried up bones sucked clean of marrow
but rattling with city-like hardness

the soft wood
petrified to stone in Seventh Street.
The train screams
warning the town of coming trouble
then moves on.

III

I walk over Seventh Street
stone at midnight
two years away from forty
and the ghosts of old friends
precede me down the street in welcome
bopping in and out of doorways
with a boogie beat
Freddie sails before me like a made-up bat
his Zorro cape just level with the stoops
he pirouettes over the garbage cans
a bundle of drugged delusions
hanging from his belt
while Joan with a hand across her throat
sings
unafraid of silence anymore
and Marion who lived on the scraps of breath
left in the refuse of strangers
searches the gutter with her nightmare eyes
tripping over the brown girl
young in her eyes and fortune
nimble as birch
and I try to recall her name
as Clement comes
smiling from a distance
his finger raised in counsel
or in blessing
over us all.

Seventh Street swells into midnight
memory ripe as a bursting grape
my head is a museum
full of other people's eyes
like stones in a dark churchyard
where I kneel praying
that my children
will not die politely
either.

April Fool Birthday Poem for Grandpa

Today is your
birthday and I have tried
writing these things before,
but now
in the gathering madness, I want to
thank you
for telling me what to expect
for pulling
no punches, back there in that scrubbed Bronx parlor
thank you
for honestly weeping in time to
innumerable heartbreaking
italian operas for
pulling my hair when I
pulled the leaves off the trees so I'd
know how it feels, we are
involved in it now, revolution, up to our
knees and the tide is rising, I embrace
strangers on the street, filled with their love and
mine, the love you told us had to come or we
die, told them all in that Bronx park, me listening in
spring Bronx dusk, breathing stars, so glorious
to me your white hair, your height your fierce
blue eyes, rare among italians, I stood
a ways off, looking up at you, my grandpa
people listened to, I stand

Poem at Thirty

it is midnight
no magical bewitching
hour for me
i know only that
i am here waiting
remembering that
once as a child
i walked two
miles in my sleep.
did i know
then where i
was going?
traveling. i'm
always traveling.
i want to tell
you about me
about nights on a
brown couch when
i wrapped my
bones in lint and
refused to move.
no one touches
me anymore.
father do not
send me out
among strangers.

44th Birthday Evening, at Harris's

Nine stories high Second Avenue
On the roof there's a party
All the friends are there watching
By the light of the moon the blazing sun
Go down over the side of the planet
To light up the underside of Earth
There are long bent telescopes for the friends
To watch this through. The friends are all in shadow.
I can see them from my bed inside my head.
44 years I've loved these dreams today.
17 years since I wrote for the first time a poem
On my birthday, why did I wait so long?
                                                        my land a good land
its highways go to many good places where
many good people were found: a home land, where song comes up
from the throat of a hummingbird & it ends
where the sun goes to across the skies of blue.
I live there with you.

My First Midnight 49th Birthday Supper

As snakes curl up the rose
base of the novena candle to
Our Lady, in 1983. Eleven years ago

tonight the mystical embrace from melodies
of Irving Berlin combine to Rhapsodies
like bail from Gary Cooper up here on the platform

Performing together the swing harmony
known as sodomy throughout our Western speaking world
thanks be to god. Happy Birthday from

Juliette Greco; and many happy returns of the day.

Toward a 44th Birthday

Mornings and eggshells crack, the eggshells scatter
to the wind. You carry them within you, the wind,
and lift your feet toward construction sites and know
that construction men eye women from the corners
of their eyes. Silence sniffs at you like a cat
and still you walk toward work, toward skyscrapers,
imagine the shattering of old plateglass. You forget
the Ko-Rec-Type, the carbon copies, the Xerox machines.
The timeclock ticks, a medallion on the wall. You dream
of grinding coffee beans, relaxing in the hot sun of Egypt,
forget that the pyramids are a wonder of the world.
Is it another vacation you need, apple trees to sit
under, the longings of a girl searching for arms,
hands to link to her tiny fingers? You sigh, reading
of diamonds in millionaires' teeth, of maids tidying
beds for other maids, of a Luckys strikebreaker being struck
by a car. No, not a car, but a driver, a human being.
What life will you find in your roamings toward China,
toward Asian America in its kitchens crowded with dreams,
on its streets teeming with cracks, toward young men
being tried for killings at the Golden Dragon, toward
pioneer women of the 19th century, the pioneer women
who live within your bones and the voice of Siu Sin Far
nudges you awake. How far, how near will sisters talk?
Will art atrophy, will it become the tools in our hands?

[1984]

The Birthday

My mind,
a child's again,
is filled with all your gifts.
I sit all night,
with the light out,
my back to the darkness
and my eyes kept focused
at one point in the light,
as though I would fix
the face and name of a friend
absent even from my memory,
as though, by fixing that spot,
I could hold its heat against
the whispers of the shadows around me.
You have smiled,
and gone off to bed,
clamping your silence down
over the brilliant surprises
you hold for me.
Now, alone in the darkness,
I recall and memorize
the cards and telegrams
that came as early and polite
as unfamiliar guests,
their eyes picking out
my wrinkles and hesitations.
I am, it seems,
between one day and another,
between one age and another,
waiting in a time when only time

itself is the gift,
waiting in a darkness
I construct for the light.
How will I measure the movement now?
How will I know at what hour
to call you,
to clear this impossible stillness?
I am, it seems,
still moving toward the first light,
a chosen point to celebrate
the fact of moving still.
Before morning, you will be here,
and all strata and all mysteries,
and the music of the moon
that will establish me here
with your one impossible gift.

A Non-Birthday Poem for My Father

Fathers never fit in poems,
and poems never please fathers.
On my father's seventieth birthday,
I tried to work him up a sonnet.
I guess I did,
and sent it off
with some kind of professional pride.
Everything seemed right.
He was seventy,
born October 25, 1896,
the numbers seemed to fit
in the proper mythological pattern.
I had my ritualistic materials,
his life, my art. Nothing could fail.
But he, with good reason,
never read my poem,
and I think he must have sat
in his small living room,
with the dying dog lying at his feet,
drowsing under the television's hum,
thinking how little I knew.
What metaphor was right
for the young boy,
fair and gray-eyed, with straight hair,
standing in the dry New Mexican evening
as his sisters offered him
the opportunity that they, black,
could never have?
Would he go off to medical school,
with Edmund Clapp shoes

and a Stetson hat,
court the high yellow princesses,
who drooled for doctors,
in a fifty dollar overcoat
and a blue serge box-back suit,
a diamond stick pin gleaming
against his shroud-like white shirt?
Not my father.
The trains would roll by at night,
the trucks would scatter cactus thorns
in their haste, big-muscled men
would knock down rocks,
and shoot a skyscraper straight to God.
Action was the tongue licking at that desert.
So he went away,
leaving his sisters to their perpetual blackness,
to find his own, or discard it,
to find his life in lines not yet laid out.
And things went fast.
A circus gig. Life in the hyped-up
masculinity of lumber camps.
He learned to drive a tractor on a boast.
And then into the New Mexico hills,
making red-eye that the feds
wouldn't bust because it always
got them there, and was clean, and safe.
Drinking and rolling drunk in the snow
with heavy women who could be Indian,
or at least, bragged that they were.
Having one son by a woman who had nine,
and leaving them both,
not really deserting them,
but not really knowing what to do
with either one of them.
And waking in the hills,
in a flurry, drunk again,
the salt used for a hangover cure

running into his eyes.
He had never seen a god,
and though he prayed at night,
whispering in his dark cabin
as he lay on the monkish cot
with his last cigarette,
he wouldn't spit near a church.
But that night he wanted
a vision and a promise,
and he got them—his own.
Out of the hills, off the juice,
straight to California and the money,
singing hillbilly songs on Central Avenue,
making love to the princesses,
who missed their doctors,
down by Wrigley Field,
taking the trolley out to San Pedro by the sea,
never to go back to the dusty black society
of New Mexico,
never to apologize to his black sisters,
lost, now, in their blackness and their dreams.
What metaphor can tell enough about the man,
stuck in credit unions, doing two shifts,
coming up with a taste for Dodges and diamond rings,
saluting with his very breath
the flags that disappear
on newly turned ships,
as they sink into the Pacific
oblivious of my father's faithfulness?
And there in the war-hurried bungalows,
new friends came up out of the south,
and he took to them, their speech,
as if it were his.
He gave them his vision,
as they sat fingering old wounds.
His son would become a doctor,
grow out of this life

it took him such pain to make.
What would you say,
when all dreams lie so magnificently,
and sisters are moaning over the coffin
of some black princess,
dead a maid, dead in the dryness
of New Mexico, having caught a chill
in a flurry in the hills, looking
for that escaped prince,
who, once, as a boy, saw visions
of a life beyond their range?
The change was never in him,
but in the monetary bursts of black sisters,
pushing forward into what was everywhere
the gift of knowing the world,
as a seasoned bear will come from winter,
tapping through his unfamiliar home,
in spring, just as the light gives him eyes,
just as the small heat burns down
the way that salt will, in snow.
It is not a metaphor my father needs,
but a way of getting down
what it means to spring from the circle,
and come back again.
It is not a metaphor my father needs,
but a way of getting down
what it means to see his son run away,
in daylight,
run away into the crowded cities,
looking for that moment
in the dry and perfumed desert of New Mexico
which the son must recreate
and see in the light of where he is,
where the father was,
and judge, not in innocence, but
standing at that point with his father,
getting down, without metaphor,

the years he cannot count,
the lives he cannot see again,
repenting the choices that sent
his black sisters, weeping,
to the grave of unwed princesses.

A Belated Birthday Poem

for Robert Dash

You are walking in the grounds
on the second day of summer
taking snapshots, the seeds
of future paintings, under
a June sun already hot
on this Sunday morning.
A red-winged blackbird sits
on the finest top (the
growing point) of a ginkgo
or maidenhair tree.
You got up at seven and went
right to work: how I envy
you your creative energy!
Painting, painting: landscapes
of Sagaponack.
You make houses out of
sheds. You cook, you
garden: how you garden!
One of the best I've ever seen.
"It's a sort of English cottage garden."
"it's a seaside garden," D. V.
flatly stated. Those dummies
what do they know? The big
thrill these past few days
is the opening of the evening primroses
—*Oenothera missourensis*, perhaps?
I love them, their lacquered
yellow petals and a touch

of orangey red. You mowed
the small field (I'd heard)
and I was worried. I like it
when the wind-bent grasses
rush right up to a house.
But you were right: how
the mowed grass (you
almost might call it a lawn)
sets off the giant shrubs
of dog roses, drenched in white
so you hardly see the green
that sets them off. Last evening
the young honey locust gleamed
against a sunset of fire
and green, blue-green. I
can't describe the color
of that tree. Imagine—
no, I can't do it. The roof
of your grand *couloir*
sprang some heavy leaks
in the last cloudburst.
It's going to cost a mint
to fix it: tar and pebbles.
It will cost a mint and where will the moola
come from? Don't worry,
it always comes, to you
at least (somehow, we get
through). I sit at the dining table
staring out at a dark pink weigela—
it's going over. For your
birthday I gave you five
of the rose Cornelia. They're
pretty shrimpy but will
grow to great shrubs, the canes
bending, studded with
many-petalled blooms: how
I wish I had the dough

to shower you with shrub
roses! But I haven't. I
sit and stare at a blue sky
lightly dashed with morning
clouds and think about
these paintings, this house,
this garden, all as beautiful
as your solitary inner life.
Your moon last night was gibbous.

DeLiza Come to London Town
A Birthday Poem for Mark

DeLiza walk across the Waterloo
at night
She short but happy that she maybe have
one inch or two
on Bonaparte
who (anyway) look peculiar up against the backdrop
of Big Ben

She cogitate
on glory and the sword/she
smoke a cigarette among a hundred homeless
white men
them the Queen forget to decorate
with bed or blanket
softening the bottomline along the lamp-lit
dirty river

DeLiza race away from Waterloo
at night
She run she clutch she hotel key real tight:
DeLiza shaken from she speculation
on The Empire and The Crown:

> Them that will not kiss the family
> like as not to kill
> the strangers that they meet

The Thirty-Eighth Year

the thirty-eighth year
of my life,
plain as bread
round as a cake
an ordinary woman.

an ordinary woman.

i had expected to be
smaller than this,
more beautiful,
wiser in afrikan ways,
more confident,
i had expected
more than this.

i will be forty soon.
my mother once was forty.

my mother died at forty-four,
a woman of sad countenance
leaving behind a girl
awkward as a stork.
my mother was thick,
her hair was a jungle and
she was very wise
and beautiful
and sad.

i have dreamed dreams
for you mama

more than once.
i have wrapped me
in your skin
and made you live again

more than once,
i have taken the bones you hardened
and built daughters
and they blossom and promise fruit
like afrikan trees.
i am a woman now.
an ordinary woman.

in the thirty-eighth
year of my life,
surrounded by life,
a perfect picture of
blackness blessed,
i had not expected this
loneliness.

if it is western,
if it is the final
europe in my mind,
if in the middle of my life
i am turning the final turn
into the shining dark
let me come to it whole
and holy
not afraid
not lonely
out of my mother's life
into my own.
into my own.

i had expected more than this.
i had not expected to be
an ordinary woman. [1974]

My Aunt Ella Meets the Buddha on His Birthday

She would like to roll down the aisles
of her church,
past the hard benches,
and in a frenzy
tell Sweet Jesus
she is holding his hand.
But though other members do,
Aunt Ella, in her soft
fried-egg body,
with two crooked fingers without nails
    (pushed into a machine in an aircraft factory during the war)
does not.

Her life,
            of course
cannot fit any testament.
Where did all the dirt come from
under the fingernails
when all she did
was try to lead a pure life.
            But a woman
            without a man
            is like a wild rose
            which blooms fast
            and flies away
            falls apart
            with the wind.
Her husband
killed in an accident

when she was like a new gardenia,
her skin white
the way girls do not like their skin to be today,
and her two daughters,
living despite her chocolate covered cherries
and true confession magazines
which warned
against all
that can happen in this world
where the innocent are butter
in a hot skillet.

Helen,
quiet,
with thick red lips and a pompadour
married a sailor
who ran off
with his Australian mistress during the war.
I was a 10 year old kid
when Helen died.
The first dead person I ever knew/or saw.
The fact that none of us knew
how she died,
leads me to believe she killed herself,
the whispers were all there
but I wasn't old enough to piece them together.
Besides,
who ever tells children about death?
It is something we must learn about from
insinuation,
the innuendos of bitterness or regret
that make people say things
they don't want to.
Something must have happened
after that day her husband's plain plump mistress
came to the door and
said she was going to have a

baby
            this I heard whispered about
            in the pantry
            between my mother and Aunt Ella.
But they didn't whisper enough
after that
for me to hear
what happened to Helen
    or her thick lips
        that could have made her some Midwestern Protestant
            relation
            to Cleopatra.

Louise,
the other daughter,
married a truck driver,
6 feet tall,
who was often out of work,
who drank,
had other women,
spawned four children who all wet the bed
and had to come and live
with Aunt Ella.
Louise was a waitress
and she and her girl friend
died of carbon monoxide poisoning
sitting in front of the cafe where they worked,
in the old car,
having a cigarette on their break.

Aunt Ella lay alone at night
in the house with four grandchildren,
reading her true confession magazine,
praying and sure that those four
teen-agers were out doing
all the things
described in her magazine.

And I'm sure they were.
They lived a life that I,
scholarly, quiet, prissy,
could only be fascinated and put off by.
Aunt Ella had a friend, whom we called Uncle Noah.
He was a secondhand junk dealer,
a man who always wore a hat, something uncommon in Southern California.
My mother told me he was very rich,
but he never spent his money.
He had been trying for years to get Aunt Ella
to marry him; but she was afraid
he might take her to bed
and try some of those things
described in the true confession magazine.
They went to church together,
but never rolled down the aisles;
though they must have shouted to God
many times;
and called on Sweet Jesus
to have compassion and some mercy
on their souls.

The title of this poem is a lie.
My aunt Ella never met the Buddha.
On his birthday, or any other time. The Buddha
scarcely ever goes where she does,
and she
doesn't like foreigners.
It is actually a common trait
in our family; none of us
really likes
foreigners.
Now isn't that down-home
American?

c. 1969

Birthday

The masques of dream—monk in his
lineage—what does he wear to shield
himself? First shield made of a cloud,
second—a tree, third—a shadow; and
leading to the stretched coils of light
(how they want to gather us up
with our permission) three men.
Two dead tho' dead is supernumerary.
The cause is the effect.
He laughed like a lake would
but only once, never twice into the same
mystery. Not ever to stop but only
to drop the baggage, to shed the
39th skin.

from *A Birthday Suite*
Happy Birthday

Happy birthday, a gray day like the first one—
You were so brave to enter our world
With its dirty rain, its look of a sepia photograph.

I call you at college, early and drowsy.
I hear you describe the party last night,
How you danced, how dancing is one of the things

You love in your life, like thinking hard. You are
All right, then, and on the telephone
Hearing the high snaredrum of your voice

I can feel you about to be born, I can feel
The barriers yield as you slide
Along the corrugated glitter,

Like some terrible rubbery ocean built of blood
That parts at a touch, leaving a path.
"What should I do," you wonder, "after I graduate?"

Now I imagine you curled under your quilt
As a cold light begins to enter
Like a knife in a pirate's teeth. Dear salt flesh,

I am ready if you are, I am afraid if you are.
I still ask: will this hurt, will it give pleasure,
Will I survive it? On your mark, get set,

We give birth to each other. Welcome. Welcome.

Paul Laurence Dunbar: 1872–1906

One hundred years of headrags, bandages,
plantation tradition gone sour;
in the smokehouse, Newport, RI
a knotted metaphor collapsed in foyer,
Miss Ann finally understanding the elevator
where you sang your standard
imperfect lyrics.

Minstrel and mask:
a landscape of speech and body
burned in verbal space,
the match cinder unstandard:
double-conscious brother in the veil—
double-conscious brother in the veil:
double-conscious brother in the veil.

—written on the 100th anniversary of his
birth, in continuum, in modality—
Dayton, Ohio: 1972

Birthday Star Atlas

Wildest dream, Miss Emily,
Then the coldly dawning suspicion—
Always at the loss—come day
Large black birds overtaking men who sleep in
        ditches.

A whiff of winter in the air. Sovereign blue,
Blue that stands for intellectual clarity
Over a street deserted except for a far-off dog,
A police car, a light at the vanishing point

For the children to solve on the blackboard
        today—
Blind children at the school you and I know
        about.
Their gray nightgowns ceased by the north wind;
Their fingernails bitten from time immemorial.

We're in a long line outside a dead-letter office.
We're dustmice under a conjugal bed carved with
        exotic fishes and monkeys.
We're in a slow-drifting coalbarge huddled
        around the television set
Which has a wire coat hanger for an antenna.

A quick view (by satellite) of the polar regions
Maternally tucked in for the long night.
Then some sort of interference—parallel lines
Like the ivory-boned needles of your
        grandmother knitting our fates together.

* * *

All things ambiguous and lovely in their
 ambiguity,
Like the nebulae in my new star atlas—
Pale ovals where the ancestral portraits have been
 taken down.
The gods with their goatees and their faint smiles

In company of their bombshell spouses,
Naked and statuesque as if entering a death camp.
They smile, too, stroke the Triton wrapped
 around the mantle clock
When they are not showing the whites of their
 eyes in theatrical ecstasy.

Nostalgias for the theological vaudeville.
A false springtime cleverly painted on cardboard
For the couple in the last row to sigh over
While holding hands which unknown to them

Flutter like bird-shaped scissors. . . .
Emily, the birthday atlas!
I kept turning its pages awed
And delighted by the size of the unimaginable;

The great nowhere, the everlasting nothing—
Pure and serene doggedness
For the hell of it—and love,
Our nightly stroll the color of silence and time.

The Author Reflects on His 35th Birthday

35 ? I have been looking forward
To you for many years now
So much so that
I feel you and I are old
Friends and so on this day , 35
I propose a toast to
Me and You
35 ? From this day on
I swear before the bountiful
Osiris that
If I ever
If I EVER
Try to bring out the
Best in folks again I
Want somebody to take me
Outside and kick me up and
Down the sidewalk or
Sit me in a corner with a
Funnel on my head

Make me as hard as a rock
35 , like the fellow in
The story about the
Big one that got away
Let me laugh my head off
With Moby Dick as we reminisce
About them suckers who went
Down with the *Pequod*
35 ? I ain't been mean enough
Make me real real mean

Mean as old Marie rolling her eyes
Mean as the town Bessie sings about
"Where all the birds sing bass"
35? Make me Tennessee mean
Cobra mean
Cuckoo mean
Injun mean
Dracula mean
Beethovenian-brows mean
Miles Davis mean
Don't-offer-assistance-when
Quicksand-is-tugging-some-poor
Dope-under-mean
Pawnbroker mean
Pharaoh mean
That's it, 35
Make me Pharaoh mean
Mean as can be
Mean as the dickens
Meaner than mean

When I walk down the street
I want them to whisper
There goes Mr. Mean
"He's double mean
He even turned the skeletons
In his closet out into
The cold"
And 35?
Don't let me trust anybody
Over Reed but
Just in case
Put a tail on that
Negro too

February 22, 1973

Birthday

And old mortality, these evening doorways into rooms,
this door from the kitchen and there's the yard,
the grass not cut and filled with sweetness,
and in the thorn the summer wounding of the sun.

And locked in the shade the dove calling down.

The glare's a little blinding still but only
for the moment of surprise, like suddenly
coming into a hall with a window at the end,

the light stacked up like scaffolding. I am
that boy again my father told not to look
at the ground so much looking at the ground.

I am the animal touched on the forehead, charmed.

In the sky the silver maple like rain in a cloud
we've tied: and I see myself walking from what looks like
a classroom, the floor waxed white, into my father's
arms, who lifts me, like a discovery, out of this life.

Happy Birthday

Thirty-three, goodbye—
the awe I feel

is not that you won't come again, or why—

or even that after
a time, we think of those who are dead

with a sweetness that cannot be explained—

but that I've read the trading-cards:
RALPH TEMPLE CYCLIST CHAMPION TRUCK RIDER

WILLIE HARRADON CYCLIST
THE YOUTHFUL PHENOMENON

F. F. IVES CYCLIST
100 MILES 6 H. 25 MIN. 30 SEC.

—as the fragile metal of their
wheels stopped turning, as they

took on wives, children, accomplishments, all those
predilections which also insisted on ending,

they could not tell themselves from what they had done.

Terrible to dress in the clothes
of a period that must end.

They didn't plan it that way—
they didn't plan it that way.

Turning Fifty

I saw the baby possum stray too far
and the alert red fox claim it
on a dead run while the mother watched,
dumb, and, oddly, still cute.
I saw this from my window
overlooking the lawn surrounded
by trees. It was one more thing
I couldn't do anything about,
though, truly, I didn't feel very much.
Had my wife been with me,
I might have said, "the poor possum,"
or just as easily,
"the amazing fox." In fact
I had no opinion about what I'd seen,
I just felt something dull
like a small door being shut,
a door to someone else's house.

That night, switching stations, I stopped
because a nurse had a beautiful smile
while she spoke about triage and death.
She was trying to tell us
what a day was like in Vietnam.
She talked about holding
a soldier's one remaining hand,
and doctors and nurses hugging
outside the operating room.
And then a story of a nineteen-year-old,
almost dead, whispering "Come closer,
I just want to smell your hair."

When my wife came home late, tired,
I tried to tell her
about the possum and the fox,
and then about the young man
who wanted one last chaste sense
of a woman. But she was interested
in the mother possum,
what did it do, and if I did anything.
Then she wanted a drink, some music
What could be more normal?
Yet I kept talking about it
as if I had something to say—
the dying boy
wanting the nurse to come closer
and the nurse's smile as she spoke
its pretty hint of pain,
the other expressions it concealed.

On Frank O'Hara's Birthday, Key West

The woman behind me at the Half Shell Bar
says "there are two anagrams for the word *fear*:
'fuck everything and run' and
'face everything and recover' and
I'm trying to do the latter"

and since it's the same with me
after my stupid heart failed and
I was life-flighted, etc. etc.,
I have to applaud the intention,

but I'm in my usual Key West glow
and loving the silliness, the tourists
at Hemingway's house photographing
the descendants of his cats.
Whenever I float in the chop
off Fort Taylor I think maybe
I'm among H_2O molecules Hemingway
or Elizabeth Bishop touched here
or O'Hara waded through off Fire Island,
perhaps not.

Where do the polished glass pebbles
on the beach come from?—lovers
long ago who smashed the bottles
on the rocks or secret drinkers
in despair? All of them say
"remember me, remember me,"
but today the huge Cuban families
come to sing and to picnic
and boom-box salsa drives the ghosts away.

I'm glad Hemingway punched Wallace Stevens
here, thus minimizing the idea of order
at Key West, and God bless the tourists
walking up and down Duval,
all they want is pleasure and some memories,
all they want is permanence and
they won't find it, though luckily
when the sun sets behind the La Concha
and the tourists applaud it and
lift their glasses in toast
the sun will come back again. In ten years
it'll be the same but they won't.

If I could comfort anyone I would
but the best I can do is remember
a sentiment of my semi-literate grandma,
who knew almost nothing beyond
cooking ("what a potato salad!") and being kind.
She said "if you remember someone you love
and you really care for them
they can never really die."

Well, she was wrong.
But because she really cared for me
she would always ask: "Are you happy?"
And I would always have to say
"Yes, I am happy. Yes, I am."

Small Waterfall: A Birthday Poem

Maybe an engineer,
stumbling on this small, all-
but-forest-swallowed waterfall—
a ten-foot drop at most—
could with some accuracy
say just how much energy
goes unharnessed here.

Enough, is it, to bring light
and heat to the one-room hut
one might
build here at its foot—where,
piercing together the *hush*
in the current's *hurl* and *crash*,
a lone man might repair
to fix a shopworn life?

Enough, anyway, to light
one image in my head: this mist-
laced column of water's
as slim as a girl's waist—
yours, say, narrow still despite
the tumble down the birth canal
of a pair of nine-pound daughters.

Well, there's nothing for it but,
sloshing my way across the pool,
I must set whimsy into fact—
which is how, one blazing, cool
August day in New Hampshire, I

come to be standing with my
arms round a cataract.

. . . Nothing new in this, it turns
out—
for I know all about embracing
a thing that flows and goes
and stays, self-propelled and -
replacing,
which in its roundabout route
carries and throws, carries and
throws
off glints at every turn, bringing

all it touches to flower
(witness those flourishing
daughters).
Your reach exceeds
my grasp, happily,
for yours is the river's power
to link with liquid, unseen threads
the low, far, moon-moved sea
and the sun's high-lit headwaters.

Birthday

You say it's your birthday
It's my birthday too, yeah
They say it's your birthday
We're gonna have a good time
I'm glad it's your birthday
Happy birthday to you

Yes we're goin' to a party party
Yes we're goin' to a party party
Yes we're goin' to a party party

I would like you to dance
Take a chance
I would like you to dance, ooo dance! Yeah

Forever Young

May God bless and keep you always,
May your wishes all come true,
May you always do for others
And let others do for you.
May you build a ladder to the stars
And climb on every rung,
May you stay forever young,
Forever young, forever young,
May you stay forever young.

May you grow up to be righteous,
May you grow up to be true,
May you always know the truth
And see the lights surrounding you.
May you always be courageous,
Stand upright and be strong,
May you stay forever young,
Forever young, forever young,
May you stay forever young.

May your hands always be busy,
May your feet always be swift,
May you have a strong foundation
When the winds of changes shift.
May your heart always be joyful,
May your song always be sung,
May you stay forever young,
Forever young, forever young,
May you stay forever young.

Birthday

Every year, on her birthday, my mother got twelve roses
from an old admirer. Even after he died, the roses kept
 coming:
the way some people lave paintings and furniture,
this man left bulletins of flowers,
his way of saying that the legend of my mother's beauty
had simply gone underground.

At first, it seemed bizarre.
Then we got used to it: every December, the house suddenly
filling with flowers. They even came to set
a standard of courtesy, of generosity—

After ten years, the roses stopped.
But all that time I thought
the dead could minister to the living;
I didn't realize
this was the anomaly; that for the most part
the dead were like my father.

My mother doesn't mind, she doesn't need
displays from my father.
Her birthday comes and goes; she spends it
sitting by a grave.

She's showing him she understands,
that she accepts his silence.
He hates deception: she doesn't want him making
signs of affection when he can't feel.

Birth

What? That spurt of sudden green,
Happy in thin sunlight
This cold April on Broadway;
The café's fogged window,
The half-seen faces, open-lipped, budding.
Their seeds roost in the dark of eyes,
The spiral passages of ears.
Come out with me!
Let's gather the flimsy stars of the words of others,
Falling God knows how, God knows where.

June 24

(for my father)

I look at the date, and it has such a look of
fullness, the fat juicy word June and then the
2 and the 4, like a couple and a couple coupled,
the whole date such a look of satiety and plenitude,
and then I remember today is your birthday,
you are 68, it is the birthday of an aging man
and yet I feel such celebration,
as if you were newborn. And it's not just the
turgid redness of your face, or your plump
fleshy hands, appealing as a baby's,
it isn't your earth-brown physical eyes
blank as a baby's lacking knowledge and memory,
it isn't just that a man of 68
is young still, you could have a child
after my own fertility is gone,
a baby dark and smart as you were
the hour of your birth, when your skin shone with the
oil of the world that lies on either
side of our world. The day moves me
because you were given back to me.
You died night after night in the years of my childhood,
sinking down into speechless torpor,
and then you were told to leave for good
and you left, for better, for worse, for a long
time I did not see you or touch you—
and then, as if to disprove the ascendancy of darkness,
little by little you came back to me
until now I have you, a living father
standing in the California sun

unwrapping the crackling caul off a cigar
and placing it in the center of his mouth
where the parent is placed, at the center of the child's life.

Birthday Poem for My Grandmother

(for L.B.M.C., 1890-1975)

I stood on the porch tonight— which way do we
face to talk to the dead? I thought of the
new rose, and went out over the
grey lawn— things really
have no color at night. I descended
the stone steps, as if to the place where one
speaks to the dead. The rose stood
half-uncurled, glowing white in the
black air. Later I remembered
your birthday. You would nave been ninety and getting
roses from me. Are the dead there
if we do not speak to them? When I came to see you
you were always sitting quietly in the chair,
not knitting, because of the arthritis,
not reading, because of the blindness,
just sitting. I never knew how you
did it or what you were thinking. Now I
sometimes sit on the porch, waiting,
trying to feel you there like the colors of the
flowers in the dark.

To Iva, Two-And-A-Half

Little fat baby, as we
don't run the world, I
wince that I can't
drive a car or a truck, ice-
skate, build shelves and
tables, ride
you up five flights of
stairs on my shoulders.
I notice you noticing
who rides most of the Big
Motorcycles, drives buses,
stacks grocery cartons, makes
loud big holes in the street.
"Mustn't hit little girls!" meaning
you, though who'd
know if we didn't say so!
Soon they'll be telling you
you can't be
Batman, Shakespeare, President, or God.
Little fat baby, going on
schoolgirl, you can be
anyone, but it won't be
easy.

Poem for Joan Fagin on Her Birthday

If the name of the inventor
could be considered a recommendation
the invention of Albert Fearnaught
Of Indianapolis, Indiana
should have had
instantaneous public acceptance.

His "Grave Signal"
patented in 1882
consisted of an elaborate device
to release a flag
through the end of a tube
which projected up
from the foot of the grave
if its occupant were
to move a hand.

For My Son

for his 30th birthday

I sit against the scarred trunk of an oak.
The sun barely windows through its branches.

Beyond a lit spot, small as a new-born's fist,
a twig quivers, then arcs toward light.

What caused such languid inclination
makes its way down the leaf: a tiny snail,

gold as corn. For an instant, they sway, lit
and in utter balance, then, in a deep bow,

the leaf releases its weight on earth and curls
back into the shade—the vitreous path

of that instant now glazed in its center.
Mathieu, if nature's cruelties know no limits,

neither do the boundaries of its grace.
I give thanks for you.

Preparing for Fifty

For Mary Rockcastle on the occasion of her 40th

It came to me that I needed a valley.
It came to me that I was done with the salmon
as my totem, how it scrapes its way upwards over rocks,
how the body quivers and strains, as if waiting
to be touched for the first time. All that is fine
for thirty, even forty, but for two years now I've believed
in fifty, someplace where who I am counts for more
than who I might become. Last week at long last,
I found a valley where I could be the small thing
for once. I could lie down in the hot springs and just be
covered. I swayed there in the water and waited
for the calm that becomes a body at fifty.
It came to me how to be at home on my back,
my genitals floating above me, an obscure species
of water lily drifting back and forth,
hardly attached to the long and clumsy root
of the body. Soothed and silenced by water, it was here
that my life has brought me, wrinkled as the day I was born.
This time around I was calmer, more sure
of how water and earth work together to offer me up
to the valley. As if I were a human sacrifice,
given up in the name of love, baptized in water, flesh
and blood in the valley of stone until the last breath.

Havana Birth

Off Havana the ocean is green this morning
of my birth. The conchers clean their knives on leather
straps and watch the sky while three couples
who have been dancing on the deck of a ship
in the harbor, the old harbor of the fifties, kiss
each other's cheeks and call it a night.

On a green velour sofa five dresses wait
to be fitted. The seamstress kneeling at Mother's feet
has no idea I am about to be born. Mother
pats her stomach which is flat
as the lace mats on the dressmaker's table. She thinks
I'm playing in my room. But as usual, she's wrong.

I'm about to be born in a park in Havana. Oh,
this is important, everything in the dressmaker's house
is furred like a cat. And Havana leans right up
against the windows. In the park, the air
is chocolate, the sweet breath of a man
smoking an expensive cigar. The grass

is drinkable, dazzling, white. In a moment
I'll get up from the bench, lured
by a flock of pigeons, lazily sipping the same syrupy
music through a straw.
Mother is so ignorant, she thinks
I'm rolled like a ball of yarn under the bed. What

does she know of how I got trapped in my life?
She thinks it's all behind her, the bloody

sheets, the mirror in the ceiling
where I opened such a sudden furious blue, her eyes
bruised shut like mine. The pigeon's eyes
are orange, unblinking, a doll's. Mother always said

I wanted to touch everything because
I was a child. But I was younger than that.
I was so young I thought whatever I
wanted, the world wanted too. Workers
in the fields wanted the glint of sun on their machetes.
Sugarcane came naturally sweet, you

had only to lick the earth where it grew.
The music I heard each night outside
my window lived in the mouth of a bird. I was so young
I thought it was easy as walking
into the ocean which always had room
for my body. So when I held out my hands

I expected the pigeon to float toward me
like a blossom, dusting my fingers with the manna
of its wings. But the world is wily, and doesn't want
to be held for long, which is why
as my hands reached out, workers lay down
their machetes and left the fields, which is why

a prostitute in a little *calle* of Havana dreamed
the world was a peach and flicked
open a knife. And Mother, startled, shook
out a dress with big peonies splashed like dirt
across the front, as if she had fallen
chasing after me in the rain. But what could I do?

I was about to be born, I was about to have
my hair combed into the new music
everyone was singing. The dressmaker sang it, her mouth
filled with pins. The butcher sang it and wiped

blood on his apron. Mother sang it and thought her body
was leaving her body. And when I tried

I was so young the music beat right
through me, which is how the pigeon got away.
The song the world sings day after day
isn't made of feathers, and the song a bird pours
itself into grows tough as a branch
lifting with the singer and the singer's delight.

Surprise

The mind dislikes surprise.
Witness the nurse of good syntax,
how she pushes her drugged charges
across the courtyard below
to the Center for Impaired Speech.

Witness the doorman hesitating
before ringing your bell to tell you
someone's on the way up.

It's why you're getting up slowly
this morning, why you don't look too closely
at the mirror, nor the coffee table
offering its testimony: the matches

crippled in their books, crushed by
the insistent pressure of thumb and forefinger,
the empty fifth, the ZigZag litter,
the pages of unclothed women, legs apart,

smiling out as if there was no danger
in this world, even from those you love.
And from those who love you in ways you have
not yet imagined—and which might surprise you,

like a style of perverse instruction
say, teaching the blind pornography,
their trained fingers hesitating above
the machined welts of braille.

It is possible to teach someone that love
is pain—by taking a fistful of hair, pulling
it up from the skull and back, till the neck
locks in place, as if breaking, till the lover
stops thinking about politics, or the five days
of fine weather—and begins to cooperate
with this gesture, applied one night
in passion, the next in pure rage.

Still, the mind is stubborn, resists
the unexpected—shuttling back and forth,
as it was taught, between similar forms—refusing
in the only way it knows how, to make sense.

So you sit this morning, while the mail comes,
and the *Times*, the phone rings and you can touch
your hair, your face, rethinking it all—

but recall your horror once
opening the front door, on your birthday, on seeing the faces
of your friends disfigured by the weight of occasion.
You thought the ones who liked you least screamed loudest:
Surprise!

For My Birthday

Home first night in years, I stand tall before the door
remembering the photo dated 1945 in windshield snow,
my father's pudgy-cheeked smile heralding my first hour.
Passing through, I waltz my mother round the kitchen

& wash her face with snow all the way from New Mexico.
Alone with his wife, I feel his presence slurp coffee
still too hot, his keys banging forgotten on his hurrying hip.
Father, I've come back to fix her storm windows

& hang the can opener within reach. I'm twenty-six today
& something has slowed in me, is more careful now.
I won't slam the door & run off to Tangier, I don't think.

My one key bangs on my hip as we turn between stove & table
five inches off the floor. Yes, I was the light going out
of you the winter night of '45, but for better or worse,
I just dropped by to say hello & waltz her once for old times.

Birthday Sonnet for Grace

I've always loved (your) Grace in 14 lines, sometimes
I have to fit my love for Grace into either
An unwieldy utopia or a smaller space,
Just a poem, not a big project for changing the world
          which I believe
It was the color of your hair that inspired me to try
          to do in words
Since such perfection doesn't exist in isolation
Like the Hyacinth, Royal or Persian blues
That go so well with you.

Now older than we were before we were forty
And working so much in an owned world for rent money
Where there seems little time for the ancient hilarity
We digressed with once on the hypnopompic verges of the sublime
Now more engrossed in hypnagogic literal mysteries of
          our age and ages I propose
To reiterate how I love you any time

1989

My Brother's Birth Day

dark, cold, the street filled with snow
against our building loud winds roared
a couple of times the door opened, almost

i shuffled the hallway mailbox wall
my mother's air groaned beside me
i was five years old, my boots tight
i waited, waited for the time to fall

my father said he'd bring back a cab
we would ride to the hospital
stay with your mother, he said
she needs you, son, be strong

my mother's breath on my neck
i didn't know i could rest my head against
whatever would happen next

Outlook

Empty bleachers
line the years.
Rain starts
like the touch
of no one
when you turn
but the cold view
of the long unlighted street,
doorways, alleys,
vacant lots,
changing stores
with ruined names,
letters askew
or missing
like teeth.

The walls collapse
as in a time-lapse film,
buildings crumble
and nothing
takes their place.
The years disperse
in swirling clouds
that race through
flickering skies
to the quickened pulse
of days and nights.

On Walt Whitman's Birthday

O strategic map of disasters, hungry America
O target for the song, the jouncing poem,
the protest
A long imperfect history shadows you
Let all suffering, toil, sex &
sublime distractions go unrecorded
Let the world continue to breathe

It's simple: a woman gets up & stretches
The world is her mirror & portal too

(Whitmanic morning task: waking the country to itself)

16 february

Linda, your birthday was the worst one. I awoke with your name on my lips but the room was already tilting and spinning. noxema cold waving hot skin my hands two red paws radiating violet threads ribs peeling intestine shuddering room rising and swelling shit and disinfectant and pale vermin burrowing. One tender moment the fever lifts the overhead fan a white propeller shifts spraying shadow across whitewashed walls shells my left arm and I drift. A child holds on to a snowflake candles illuminate your trusting face. happy birthday my sister, syrupy hairs stick to my cheek purple spine merging plastic sheet. happy birthday sister, I reach relief my burnoose yards of cheesecloth cocoon to roll up in water a distant pitcher liquid streaming golden stars so aware of teeth and temples and the heat avenging moving in like squatter laughing with huge white teeth like tombstone and so aware of the temple on the hill surrounded by jackangels.

hotel internacional mexico
16.2.74

Imported Days

some days, like birthdays, are imported
from france, honolulu and bangkok.
you stretch them out by minutes
and enjoy every piece
while buildings bury themselves in the ground.
you row in and out of a mailman,
a cosmic mailman
from the african or indian market of birthdays.
the sky of this has a hole in the middle,
it pours feasts!
never again beyond into the banal

At 102, Romance Comes Once A Year

(for Joseph Johnson, Seattle)

down in Banyantown where young
girls prance swaybacked
for strangers we hear tell
some folks be rememberin' how
old men used to work till
they nothin' more than corn
cobs of brown skin waitin'
for the holiday sun
to warm them red

upriver houses don't need much
care so the old men sit
by the shore where eddies
of water churn the air fresh
and they can munch over
annual events and how too
many young girls go
bad all th' time now

when hours paint houses sunset
orange, old men who be still tryin'
to learn what the word *retire*
means to somebody who ain't never
been laid off uy forgettin'
their strokes and force angry
limbs to stiffly water lawns
while their gummy eyes
watch some woman's skirt sway

no matter where I go, Joseph
they all remind me of you
with your shoeshine stand and 100
birthdays but still not looking
a day over 65 by any real
calendar and as pretty black
as any woman be wantin'
noddin' yes when I whisper
magic names of lost cities:
Montego, Toberua, Titicaca, Tiv
Tupelo, Topeka, Tacoma

Mother at Eighty

You come in dream, Mother, or not at all,
distressed by drugs, scattering quips, complaining
still about the way they torture you. Married late,
you wouldn't leave the party, forced Hawaii
to its knees; I've seen the cascades of your hair,
heard the devilish laugh each suitor ducked, ricocheting
through the rooms; a wastrel girl, uncontrollable.
And press through time to take you in my arms,
to find you now, coldcocked by suffering,
baggage in a train that's plowed its way
into the dark and snowy woods, and stopped.
I see you there, my dreamer, nodding at your window,
unacknowledged, except perhaps by the spotted dog
limping in the snow, that sees you lift your head,
and trembles in your smoky, avid glance.

On a Shared Birthday: J. C. L. 1953–1979

Now with another year I save
his battered case with the driller's glove
and spearmint gum, salt worn, stiff—
the modern sailor's two week stint
in the pull for oil out in the Gulf.
Roughnecker's gig of bad food, bad sleep,
the six hour drive down Louisiana's spine,
rain all the way to the measured
whistle of daywork, nightwork,
work and wake at 3 a.m. And I see again
what I never saw: my brother timing the seconds against
losing his hand as he centers the steel
under the hammer's flying weight
that jams the rod into the ocean floor . . .

I pull myself up,
back to dawn and the single bird note, sustained
stop and start like worry.
Face into sheet, I nag
red-winged blackbird, more naming
to sidestep panic, as if that whistle
could make sense of a life that's missing.
What's this birthday now
but the baggage of injury and pardon—
two landscapes and one bird
crossing them night after night.
Where, where, where, it sings,
is your brother now? In this dream
no death, no murderer's

hand on my brother's throat. No body
dumped in the convenient swamp, the convenient rain
that goes on washing away.
The litany of what we'll never know
comes to nothing but the haunting in one bird's song.

A Birthday Story (Math in Hollywood)

J. is giving his reading
but just before he begins
he tells us a dream he's had:
it's a reading, he's about to
read, but it's his birthday
party too, and he calls it
as if it is in capitals his
Childhood Birthday Party.
Soon everyone leaves, but is
only downstairs, as if to make
it rougher, sadder. A tall
and truly great Syracuse basketball
player takes their place, but
even though he is famous he
cannot replace J.'s sadness
and J.'s friends. The J. in
J. smiles, the reading begins.

*

J. tells me another dream
a few days later: we're in my
office: I tell him before he
starts he ought to write down
what is now the above dream:
it's above average: something
in my syntax interests him:
he tells me the same: to write
"it" down: I'm thinking too of
D. H. Lawrence's confusing-to-me

Name Day Party in *Women in Love:*
I almost managed to fail that
course twice I received so many
extensions: I failed it once:
another at the same time: I was
a senior and not about to head
to war: now I am a *senior* to some
and I feel like I've been at war:
my chest hurts, I'm living for
someone other than myself: this
is hard on one and harder when
one doesn't honestly know who one
is living for: it's confusing too
like math in Hollywood which I
also failed: 4 times, no joking:
the 5th time I did pass but also
passed on to Hollywood just a
few years later: that was also
a war, minor: the sign really
read "Elvis doesn't live here any-
more"—What was I thinking? What
did one have in mind? A year later
it's Lawrence and Joyce and the "minor"
Russians: and CO status and pregnant
time and word wars: somewhere in
this fragment of re-collecting
I've left J. and me and my love
of the writer J. and whatever I
was supposed to say somewhere in
the dust: so be it: it is not my
birthday but it is the birth of
a day: it is the last Sunday in
February in the 20th Century: only
thought of that now: it's raining
and gray: think of John Weiners'
line: What will one do, how?

Nicole at Thirteen

Grace on which we fix our gaze; pillar
of light that is her lithe, gymnast's
body.
You and I have already passed
the threshold on which she pauses—
how beautiful the naked foot poised
in air.
We've already entered the sexual
dark and now stare back at her, still
standing there as if she could hold
that pose forever.
Her bright body
in the doorway—white, lit candle;
our thralled, animal eyes
flashing back from the dark beyond.

Fiftieth Birthday

Only less sure of all I never knew.
Always more awed by what is never new.
Computer, spare the mustang's randomness.

There was an oracle. On Samothrace?
There have been tablets. Here? Some greener place?
I (leaf) paint leaves that (falling) try to dance.

Have seen the big death, felt the little death:
The icy and the April breathlessness.
And understand them less and less and less.

Have met the loam-fed and the plastic wreath:
Statesman and hack. Two frightening frightened boys.
Both more endearing than the consequence.

Have heard your rebels and have heard your guild:
And still can't tell the standard from the stance
When both are so rehearsed a cheering noise.

Have squandered silver and have hoarded pence.
Have watched the ant-hill build, burn up, rebuild
(The running is and isn't meaningless)

At Ilium. Or will it be South Bend?
I'll grudge the run a meaning in the end
When wounds that might wound back or else "transcend"

Have risked—instead—to be. Not even bless.

1966

June 11

It's my birthday I've got an empty
stomach and the desire to be
lazy in the hammock and maybe
go for a cool swim on a hot day
with the trombone in Sinatra's
"I've Got You Under My Skin"
in my head and then to break for
lunch a corned-beef sandwich and Pepsi
with plenty of ice cubes unlike France
where they put one measly ice cube
in your expensive Coke and when
you ask for more they argue with
you they say this way you get more
Coke for the money showing they
completely misunderstand the nature of
American soft drinks which are an
excuse for ice cubes still I wouldn't
mind being there for a couple of
days Philip Larkin's attitude
toward China comes to mind when
asked if he'd like to go there he said
yes if he could return the same day

December 9th

I have the same
birthday as John
Milton. Did
you know that?
So I don't have to
write long poems about
heaven & hell—everything's
been lost in my lifetime
& I'm usually blind drunk
and not so serious
either. However . . .
when I am nearly dead
will you read to me
in bed? Will you pre-
tend to be my daughter
or my wife, Whoever,
will you crawl in
& die with Me?

1982

Enid at 70

once the world was as large as your breasts
shelter and safety were in your arms
now i seek protection and the world turns away
i think of lincoln walking alone in the white house
a civil war outside and young men embracing death
you are my mother a widow at seventy

Turning Forty in the 90s

April 1990

We promised to grow old together, our dream
since years ago when we began
to celebrate our common tenderness
and touch. So here we are:

Dry, ashy skin, falling hair, losing breath
at the top of stairs, forgetting things.
Vials of Septra and AZT line the bedroom dresser
like a boy's toy army poised for attack—
your red, my blue, and the casualties are real.

Now the dimming in your man's eyes and mine.
Our bones ache as the muscles dissolve,
exposing the fragile gates of ribs, our last defense.
And we calculate pensions and premiums.
You are not yet forty-five, and I
not yet forty, but neither of us for long.

No Senior discounts here, so we clip coupons
like squirrels in late November, foraging
each remaining month or week, day or hour.
We hold together against the throb and jab
of yet another bone from out of nowhere poking through.
You grip the walker and I hobble with a cane.
Two witnesses for our bent generation.

Poem on My Son's Birthday

At dawn
on the window sill
it's watery trees it's light
it's just hanging there waiting

poetry

I want to walk   you can come or
you can sleep or
you can dream of walking someplace better

and that still means we're not together

    except today
    one more day   (you were born)

It's a communion
you can hardly see
a kind of reunion   just a little one

you and me.

A Good Day

Saturday.
Freckled leaves after rain,
water pools sprinkled like paw prints
over the road.
With bare feet
my heart dips
into the rainbow
by the red doud.
My dog
shakes water from his fur,
I shiver with wild joy!

I rise,
swing my porch door open
to break the intolerable calm
between myself and the poem
I am working on.
A robin swirls
haltingly into the screenless door,
wings frantically beating
backflight at seeing me,
as my own soul does
at seeing itself
before the blank paper.

A check arrived in the afternoon mail.
To celebrate, we go to a second-hand store
and buy a lime-green patio set.
On the front porch,
beneath the green/white striped Italian umbrella,

Beatrice and I sip cappuccino.
Our Irish setter Kianne
slumps in the unmown front yard grass, auburn
lump of burred rug, nip-teasing
a dead black duck
dragged in from fields across the road.
Light that left stars millions of years ago
reaches us now
and blesses my brow.

Turning Thirty, I Contemplate Students Bicycling Home

This is the weather of change
and clear light. This is
weather on its B side,
askew, that propels
the legs of young men
in tight jeans wheeling
through the tired, wise
spring. Crickets too
awake in choirs
out of sight, although
I imagine we see
the same thing
and for a long way.

This, then, weather
to start over.
Evening rustles
her skirts of sulky
organza. Skin
prickles, defining
what is and shall not be. . . .

How private
the complaint of these
green hills.

Wingfoot Lake
(Independence Day, 1964)

On her 36th birthday, Thomas had shown her
her first swimming pool. It had been
his favorite color, exactly—just
so much of it, the swimmers' white arms jutting
into the chevrons of high society.
She had rolled up her window
and told him to drive on, fast.

Now this *act of mercy*: four daughters
dragging her to their husbands' company picnic,
white families on one side and them
on the other, unpacking the same
squeeze bottles of Heinz, the same
waxy beef patties and Salem potato chip bags.
So he was dead for the first time
on Fourth of July—ten years ago

had been harder, waiting for something to happen,
and ten years before that, the girls
like young horses eyeing the track.
Last August she stood alone for hours
in front of the T.V. set
as a crow's wing moved slowly through
the white streets of government.
That brave swimming

scared her, like Joanna saying
Mother, we're Afro-Americans now!
What did she know about Africa?

Were there lakes like this one
with a rowboat pushed under the pier?
Or Thomas' Great Mississippi
with its sullen silks? (There was
the Nile but the Nile belonged
to God.) Where she came from
was the past, 12 miles into town
where nobody had locked their back door,
and Goodyear hadn't begun to dream of a park
under the company symbol, a white foot
sprouting two small wings.

Birthday

You hitch into the city
and walk a few blocks
until you find a small
hotel you can afford.
If you didn't have to leave
the next day, you'd offer
to paint it since you need
the work—tell the owner
to buy enough for two coats
but brush the second onto
yourself because it's getting cold
and there's only a sweater
in your suitcase.

The manager behind the desk
has a cigar stuck in the side
of his mouth like a cork,
his bald head shining—
waxed the way the floor
needs to be. When you can't
remember your name, you pick
another just as good, sign in
then ask him if he knows
when the first bus leaves
in the morning. He says forget it
since the cheapest ride in town
is the next woman he can send
up to your room in 15 minutes.

You take the elevator

to the 4th floor, open the door
to 407, check out the bed,
chair and sink before flipping
on the switch. A bulb hanging
from a wire lights up
like an idea you're glad
even you never had.

Throwing your suitcase on
the bed, you walk over
to look out the window.
An apartment light two blocks over
goes on and lights the top
of a water tower shaped like a candle
on the warehouse across the street.
It reminds you today
is your birthday and when
a switch or wind blows
the apartment light out
you close your eyes and make
a wish.

Birthday Dream

For Pam, 33 years now

Tomorrow is another gray ocean
Rising up through the heart
Of a mountain flower extending
Out across the cliffs and rocks
In the turquoise of my dreams.

In an instant, I recall
The daydream whispers
Of my past mixed with
The calmness of your love
Draping my selfish spirit
Regal and alive. The blueness
Of a cool shadow lifts
Itselfabove your scarlet wreath
Of warmth and sunshine.

Aware in the pleasant
Waves of your heart, I
Float freely on a high tide
Of your innocent love. A lighthouse
Calling me away from
The brokenness of my self.

I make this promise
Now, right here, on the front porch,
I will never return to my old life;
An old curse that has kept me
Inside a house of loneliness and ego.

John Kennedy Jr. at Twenty-One

John, his mother and sister step from
the black limousine. They're lit brighter
than everyone else by a round of flashes
and glare off the mini-cam kliegs. He
bites his lip. "This again." Friends
of the family clear a path to the grave.
Once they've knelt, the crowd of re-
porters shouts some condolences. John
thinks they're lying, even the veterans
he remembers from Washington. He grips
his mother's arm. "Mom," he whispers,
"let's make this brief." She nods and
on that motion's down swing her neck
crumples up. The cameras click. She's
fifty-one. Her cross, breathy mouth
says, "Yes," with the *s* held forever it
seems. She's annoyed. Caroline stares
straight ahead, swearing out of one
side of her mouth. Later in A.P. wire
photos she'll seem stoned out and the
rumors will start. But here lies one
shimmering nameplate piled with their
world's paltry backyard of flora. John
looks at the flowers, his knees, his
nails. He listens to what the report-
ers are babbling. He lowers his head.
The platform's imperiously gray, just
the way the storm left it. His knees
are soaked through with water. His
eyes are left cold by the long walk

from him to their reason for being
blue. When he returns to his feet at
his mother's command and starts back
to the car his head's ducked. One
hand's drawn in front of his face so
the cameras can't pick his thoughts.
They're impenetrable but they will
not be glossed over, unlike the grass.

For My Birthday

After much talk and laughter
friends are buying a whore,
one I couldn't worm from
the bars with a toothy smile.
He will be fairly beautiful.
They have shopped the foul
alleys of Selma, finding red
hair and eyes with dark powers.
On the night of my birth I'll
proceed to a particular motel.
At an appointed moment someone
will knock two times and enter.
It will be my gift, paid up
until morning, and I'll try
to talk with him first, then
just give up and rattle him
orders that he'll understand
or embellish, teaching me love
the easy way: arms obligated
to take me, repaying each kiss,
caressing by reflex. I'll be
nice to him, hoping he might
contract my desire, knowing he'll
ditch me when his watch strikes
day, anxious for a real fuck or
someone who speaks his language,
as dull and slurred as that is.

Relic

It must've been some occasion—
the Granddad's birthday, maybe—
because all the family,
brothers, cousins, wives and kids,
took the afternoon fishing at the reservoir
that now covered the southwest quarter.
Years back he and his boys had been warned
of the planned flooding, had cashed
the Feds' check issued for their land,
then watched from their tractors
as hundreds of trucked-in workers in fancy rigs
shifted the bluffs year by year
till the massive earthen dam altered
even the weather, and bred mosquitoes there.
Grandma died a month before the first fields
went under, and just once the old man snapped
he was glad she didn't see it;
as little was said afterward of the lost land
as of her. Now the men baited lines
for the boys to cast, children waded
where the women could see them,
sandwiches and tea were unpacked,
pike after glittering pike was reeled in.
The treeless bank continued its quiet surrender
to the reservoir, unremarked,
and late in the afternoon one of the little ones
dredged up from the sand between her toes
a perfect rose quartz arrowhead
they passed from hand to hand.

The Birthday Party

The children flew in a state
of panic through the house—
among sixty white houses, all alike,
which someone had called
without humor, "a development."
There were the baby and his sister
and the neighbor's kids.
No one asked where the grown-ups were.
They galloped on the furniture
and played at being wild Indians.
The mother of the birthday girl
was sad enough to die,
and one week later she would try it—
her daughter too small to unlock the door
so the police would have to break it down
while she stood screaming in the living room—
but now she ran among the others, in a party dress,
till the mother said tiredly
she guessed it was time to send the children home,
and the party stopped a moment, in its tracks.
"But where's the cake?"
"We haven't had our cake!"—a new fear
trilling in the voice. And yes, there it was,
with thick, pink icing, and someone
dimmed the lights. There was a hush,
the candles lit, the birthday song
and something sweet. The children grew solemn,
bowed their heads like beggar-monks,—
then they pushed back their chairs. It seemed
too little and too late, but to the children
just enough, and they went
shouting happily out into the daylight.

Birthday

I make my way down the back stairs
in the dark. I know
it sounds crude to admit it,
but I like to piss in the back yard.

You can be alone for a minute
and look up at the stars,
and when you return
everyone is there.

You get drunker, and listen to records.
Everyone agrees.
The dead singers have the best voices.
At four o'clock in the morning

the dead singers have the best voices.
And I can hear them now,
as I climb the stairs
in the dark I know.

On The Birthday

Not being equal to the dead
And what was expected, the tree
Becomes a sign I pass of how
It has gone on long enough,

Branches hold up the beginning
Stars like waiting candles. I learn
To live with less
And less beauty while the child sleeps

Believing she is already
Home. Out of her hand falls one shoe,
Her mouth stained with whatever kind
Of paradise she has wished for

And something I had in mind
Darts across the road, a small animal
Moving perfectly between tires
As I look back to see nothing has changed.

Birthday Poem

Does the road wind past fields?
Silver in the rotted cups of fenceposts, snow
or moonlight; you no longer know the season.
Are the answers whole? Words are gravel
spinning from a tire. Your name? Forgotten,
or simply left behind in the long minnow's pull
through tunnels where your hair turns white; your voice,
receding, twists back into your mother's veins.
Color that has stained the nasturtiums
and thickened like a bruise on the eggplants
lifts from the garden at dusk, taken back
into the sun. Who is the sun?
Nothing now but particles of red or gold
in someone's else's eye it grows
toward moonlight on a road
where gravel glistens.
A radio plays in a deserted parking lot
in the all-night laundromat's blue glare.

Birth Day

For Alexandra, born May 17, 1999

Armored in red, her voice commands
every corner. Bells gong on squares,
in steeples, answering the prayers.
Bright tulips crown the boulevards.

Pulled fiom the womb she imitates
that mythic kick from some god's head.
She roars, and we are conquered.
Her legs, set free, combat the air.

Naked warrior: she is our own.
Entire empires are overthrown.

Birthday

When Cortez burned Mexico City,
the stars glittered black in the sky
before the centuries of white light,
four million birds scorched in the Aztec aviaries,
the conquistadores laughing as their torches
set the moon of feathers on fire,
the stench turning the lake into the next world,
clouds of amber calling to the birds
to come alive centuries later, rolling across
the city as if water could rise without wings,
without the centuries of white light
touching everything that flew.

I saw the burning city
several weeks after my birthday.
I flew overhead in a plane,
looked down at the streets
I had known long ago.
The burning city ate itself,
miles of smoke and fire cleaning
what had refused to go.
I passed overhead in a metallic cloud,
unidentified witness to what was lost.
Several memories of love.
A few old photos of the cliff dwellings.
Dreams written down, changed to hide the fear.
Voices calling in a new language.
Two or three paths to the ultimate wall.

* * *

When Cortez burned Mexico City,
brown faces came out of the water,
fled naked toward the heart never sacrificed,
four millions birds falling into great mounds
of breathing earth, taking their time
vanishing from my swollen hands.
When I burned the house of my father,
the color red turned brown, gave me time
to come back. When I burned
the house of my father, no one was there.
No one knew I was there.
I loved the burning city
several months after my birthday.

She Thinks of Him on Her Birthday

It's still winter,
and still I don't know you
anymore, and you don't know

me. But this morning I stand
in the kitchen with the illusion,
peeling a clementine. Each piece

snaps like the nickname for a girl,
the tinny bite it was
to be one once. Again I count

your daughters and find myself in the middle,
the waist of the hourglass,
endlessly passed through and passed through

but holding nothing, dismayed
by the grubby February sun
I was born under and the cheap pleasure

it gives the window. Yet I raise the shade
for it, and try not to feel it is wrong
to want spring, to be a season

further from you—not wrong to wish
for a hard rain, a hard wind
like one we sat out in together
or came in from together.

Birthday Song

The day I was born I was
born screaming, weren't we all,
and who's to say there was no reason
to crawl headfirst into that vastness,
the great cathedral of what if.
I was alone and wanting and pissed off.
I felt the wind moving through it,
the sheer fact of desire entering
me like a long breath, obvious
as candlelight and cheap wine,
while happiness insinuated itself,
little flaws in the flesh.
Then one day it's ten minutes past the time
anything matters, and someone
is stepping closer through
the music, cutting slow circles
across the bright prairie
of dancing, moving among the loud
shirts and soft eyes of the newly lost.
And I can feel myself falling
like hard luck, like some poor excuse
for rain, or every notion that takes me
unawares, miles from everything,
knowing full well whatever fate
befalls me, gravity takes me
by the heart and sleeve.
Imagine a bed made for such
forced landings, the slow tumble
out of our own survival instincts, feathers
and grief, night falling where it will,

going down like barometric pressure,
while life plays like a blue movie
on somebody's dirty little bedroom wall
And love still shines like the hall light
across those perfect ruins, a train
wreck of misspent youth and joy
and doing it all over, with anyone,
while spread eagle loneliness
rubs its sore ankles on God's infernal kitchen floor, black
square, white
square, the music careening over
everything broken, and rising,
and newly born.
Imagine someone moving closer
through that music, shrugging off
the wings unbuttoning
the losses, then bending to touch
the tender corners of the cloth,
thinking how easily
we could erase the years
gleaming on the table
with one eternal breath of praise
that puts out each small fire
as if it were a wish
and we were singing.

index

symbols

16 february, 172
44th Birthday Evening, at Harris's, 116
49th Birthday Trip (What Are You On?), 76
65, 8

-a-

Aging, 39
Althaus, Keith, 170
Ammons, A. R., 82
Appleman, Phillip, 89
April Fool Birthday Poem for Grandpa, 114
At 102, Romance Comes Once A Year, 174–175
At Sixty, 92
Author Reflects on His 35th Birthday, 141–142

-b-

Baca, Jimmy Santiago, 188–189
Belated Birthday Poem, 126–128
Berrigan, Ted, 116
Berryman, John, 37
Bidart, Frank, 144
Bight [On my birthday], 28–29
Birth (Hughes), 11
Birth (Zweig), 154
Birth Day, 204
Birthday (Creeley), 80–81
Birthday (Gluck), 153
Birthday (Gonzalez), 205–206
Birthday (Harrison), 136
Birthday (Ignatow), 40
Birthday (Lennon & McCartney), 151
Birthday (Pilkington), 193–194
Birthday (Plumly), 143
Birthday (Stern), 67–68
Birthday (Wright), 119–120
Birthday (Wright), 201
Birthday Cake, 30
Birthday Candle, 70
Birthday Card for a Psychiatrist, 50–51
Birthday Dream (Dickey), 52–53
Birthday Dream (Liebler), 195
Birthday Memorial to Seventh Street, 110–113
Birthday Party (Jacobsen), 31–32
Birthday Party (Rosenberg), 200
Birthday Poem (Brunk), 203
Birthday Poem (Defress), 48
Birthday Poem (Hecht), 55–57
Birthday Poem (Knight), 103–104
Birthday Poem (Kumin), 79
Birthday Poem for My Grandmother, 157
Birthday Poem for My Little Sister, 61–62
Birthday Poem to My Wife, 82
Birthday Present, 106–108
Birthday Song, 208–209

Birthday Sonnet, 13
Birthday Sonnet for Grace, 168
Birthday Star Atlas, 139–140
Birthday Story (Math in Hollywood), 179–180
Birthdays, 25
Birthplace, 5
Bishop, Elizabeth, 28–29
Black, Sophie Cabot, 202
Booth, Philip, 73–74
Bosselaar, Laure-Ann, 160
Boyle, Kay, 12
Brunk, Juanita, 203
Burkard, Michael, 179–180

-c-

Carroll, Jim, 187
Ciardi, John, 44–46
Clifton, Lucille, 130–131
Coleman, Robert H., 3
Cooper, Denis, 196–198
Cordescu, Andrei, 173
Corso, Gregory, 99–101
Creeley, Robert, 80–81
Cummings, E.E., 8
Curbelo, Silvia, 208–209

-d-

Davison, Peter, 92
December 9th, 184
Defress, Madeline, 48
Deliza Come to London Town—A Birthday Poem for Mark, 129
Denby, Edwin, 13
Dickey, James, 52–53
Diprima, Diane, 114
Dixon, Melvin, 186
Dove, Rita, 190–192
Dugan, Alan, 54
Dunn, Stephen, 145–146
Dylan, Bob, 152

-e-

Early April Morning, 10
Elroy, Colleen, 174–175
Enid at 70, 185

-f-

February Twelfth Birthday Statement, 54
Field, Edward, 61–62
Fiftieth Birthday, 182
First Day Of The Future, 91
Fitzgerald, Robert, 26
Five Words for Joe Dunn on His 22nd Birthday, 77–78
For a Thirteenth Birthday, 63–65
For Helene On Her 30th Birthday, 97–98
For Lucy, *On Her Birthday*, 102
For Marianne Moore's Birthday, 12
For My Birthday (Cooper), 198
For My Birthday (Schultz), 167
For My Son, 160
Forever Young, 152
from *A Birthday Suite* (Happy Birthday), 137
Frost, Robert, 5

-g-

Garrison, Deborah, 207
Gift for My Mother's 90th Birthday, 49
Ginsberg, Allen, 87–88
Gluck, Louise, 153
Gonzalez, Ray, 205–206
Good Day, 188–189
Goodman, Paul, 30
Gregory, Horace, 10

-h-

Hacker, Marilyn, 158
Happy Birthday, 1
Happy Birthday (Bidart), 144
Happy Birthday Party Song, 2

Happy Birthday to You—A Short History of the Most Popular Song in the World, 3
Harper, Michael S., 138
Harris, Sam H., 4
Harrison, Jim, 136
Havana Birth, 162–164
Hayden, Robert, 35–36
Hecht, Anthony, 55–57
Hill, Mildred J., 1–4
Hill, Patty Smith, 1–4
Howes, Barbara, 38
Hughes, Langston, 11

-i-

I am 25, 101
Ignatow, David, 40
Imported Days, 173
In the Winter of My Thirty-Eighth Year, 90

-j-

Jacobsen, Josephine, 31–32
Jarrell, Randall, 39
John Button Birthday, 83–84
John Kennedy Jr. at Twenty-One, 196–197
Jordan, June, 129
June 11, 183
June 24th (for my father), 155–156
Justice, Donald, 70

-k-

Kaherawak's Birthday-July 28, 95–96
Kenny, Maurice, 95–98
Kinnell, Galway, 91
Kizer, Carolyn, 59–60
Knight, Etheridge, 103–105
Koch, Kenneth, 69
Kumin, Maxine, 79
Kunitz, Stanley, 14–15

-l-

Lehman, David, 183
Lennon, John, 151
Letthauser, Brad, 149–150
Liebler, M. L., 195
Lighting Your Birthday Cake, 89
Lines on His Birthday, 58
Logan, John, 58
Lorde, Audre, 110–113
Lowell, Robert, 47

-m-

Mathis, Cleopatra, 177–178
Mayer, Bernadette, 168
McCartney, Paul, 151
Meehan, Maud, 49
Menashe, Samuel, 75–76
Merwin, W.S., 90
Middle Age, 47
Millay, Edna St. Vincent, 9
Miller, E. Ethelbert, 185
Miller, Vassar, 66
Mitchell, Susan, 162–164
Moore, James, 161
Morley, Hilda, 42–43
Moss, Stanley, 71–72
Mother at Eighty, 176
Moving In, 33–34
Mueller, Lisel, 63–65
Muske, Carol, 165–166
My Aunt Ella Meets the Buddha on His Birthday, 132–135
My Brother's Birth Day, 169
My First Midnight 49th Birthday Supper, 117
Myles, Eileen, 184

-n-

Nicole at Thirteen, 181
Non-Birthday Poem for My Father, 121–125
Nystrom, Debra, 199

- o -

Ochester, Ed, 147–148
October, 35–36
Ode: My 24th Year, 87–88
O'Hara, Frank, 83–86
Olds, Sharon, 155–157
On Birthday of Kenneth's, 86
On a Shared Birthday: J. C. L. 1953–1979, 177–178
On Approaching My Birthday, 66
On Frank O'Hara's Birthday, Key West, 147–148
On My Birthday, 75
On the Birthday, 202
On Walt Whitman's Birthday, 171
Only Card I Got on My Birthday Was from an Insurance Man, 41
Orr, Gregory, 181
Ostriker, Alicia, 137
Outlook, 170

- p -

Padgett, Ron, 159
Paschen, Elyse, 204
Passing Through, 14–15
Patchen, Kenneth, 27
Paul Laurence Dunbar: 1872–1906, 138
Pilkington, Kevin, 193–194
Plath, Sylvia, 106–108
Plumly, Stanley, 143
Poem at Thirty, 115
Poem for a Certain Lady on Her 33rd Birthday, 105
Poem for Joan Fagin on Her Birthday, 159
Poem for My 20th Birthday, 69
Poem for My Thirty-Ninth Birthday, 44–46
Poem for Your Birthday, 59–60
Poem on My Birthday, 71–72
Poem on My Son's Birthday, 187
Preparing for Fifty, 161

- r -

Reed, Ishmael, 141–142
Relic, 199
Rosenberg, Liz, 200

- s -

Safety at Forty: or, an Abecedarian Takes a Walk, 93–94
Sanchez, Sonia, 115
Schultz, Philip, 167
Schuyler, James, 126–128
Shapiro, Karl, 33–34
She Thinks of Him on Her Birthday, 207
Silver Age Song, 26
Simic, Charles, 139–140
Sissman, L.E., 93–94
Sixty-six, 73–74
Small Waterfall: A Birthday Poem, 149–150
Smith, Charlie, 176
Smith, Patti, 172
Spicer, Jack, 77–78
Stafford, William, 41
Stefan—A Last Birthday Poem, 42–43
Stern, Gerald, 67–68
Stevens, Wallace, 7
Surprise, 165–166

- t -

Thirty-Eighth Year, 130–131
To a Little Girl, One Year Old, In a Ruined Fortress, 16–24
To Be Recited to Flossie on Her Birthday, 6
To Canada (For Washington's Birthday), 85
To Iva, Two-And-A-Half, 158
To Jesus on His Birthday, 9
To W.H. Auden on his Fiftieth Birthday, 38

Toward a 44th Birthday, 118
Turning Fifty, 145–146
Turning Forty in the 90s, 186
Turning Thirty, I Contemplate Students Bicycling Home, 190

- u -

Updike, John, 109
Upon the Last Day of His Forty-Ninth Year, 109

- v -

Van Duyn, Mona, 50–51
Verga, Angelo, 169
Viereck, Peter, 182

- w -

Wakoski, Diane, 132–135
Waldman, Anne, 171
Warren, Robert Penn, 16–24
Weiners, John, 117
What Splendid Birthdays, 27
What We See Is What We Think, 7
Williams, Miller, 102
Williams, William Carlos, 6
Wingfoot Lake (Independence Day, 1964), 191–192
Wolfert, Helen, 25
Wong, Nelle, 118
Wright, Franz, 201
Wright, Jay, 119–125
Writ on the Eve of My 32nd Birthday (a slow thoughtful spontaneous poem), 99–100

- y -

Your Birthday in Wisconsin You Are 140, 37

- z -

Zweig, Paul, 154

permissions

Keith Althaus, "Outlook." Reprinted with the permission of the author.
R. Ammons, "Birthday Poem to My Wife." Copyright © by A. R. Ammons. Reprinted with the permission of the Estate of A. R. Ammons.
Philip Appleman, "Lighting Your Birthday Cake" from *New and Selected Poems 1956–1996.*
Copyright © 1996 by Philip Appleman. Reprinted with the permission of the University of Arkansas Press.
Jimmy Santiago Baca, "A Good Day," from Black Mesa Poems. Copyright © 1989. Reprinted with permission of New Directions Publishing Corporation.
Ted Berrigan, "44th Birthday Evening, at Harris's" from *Selected Poems.* Copyright © 1964 by Ted Berrigan. Copyright 8 2000 by Alice Notley. Reprinted with the permission of Viking Penguin, a division of Penguin Putnam Inc.
John Berryman, "Your Birthday in Wisconsin You Are 140" from *Delusions, etc.* Copyright ©1972 by John Berryman. Reprinted with the permission of Farrar, Straus & Giroux, Inc..
Frank Bidart, "Happy Birthday" from *In the Western Night: Collected Poems 1965–1990.* Copyright © 1990 by Frank Bidart. Reprinted with the permission of Farrar Straus & Giroux, Inc..
Elizabeth Bishop." The Bight,:" from The Complete Poems, 1927–1979. Copyright © 1980 by Alice Helen Methfessel. Reprinted with permission of Farrar, Straus & Giroux, LLC.
Sophie Cabot Black. " On The Birthday." Reprinted with permission of the author.
Philip Booth, "Sixty-three" from *Lifelines: Selected Poems 1950–1999.* Copyright © 1999 by Phillip Books. Reprinted with the permission of Viking Penguin, a division of Penguin Putnam Inc.
Laure-Ann Bosselaar, "For My Son" from *Small Gods of Grief.* Copyright © 2001 by Laure-Ann Bosselaar. Reprinted with the permission of BOA Editions, Ltd.

Kay Boyle, "For Marianne Moore's Birthday" from *Testament for My Students and Other Poems*. Copyright © 1970 by Kay Boyle. Reprinted with the permission of Copper Canyon Press, PO Box 271, Port Townsend, WA 98368-0271.

Juanita Brunk, "Birthday Poem" from *Brief Landings On Earth's Surface*. Copyright © 1996 by Juanita Brunk. Reprinted with the permission of The University of Wisconsin Press.

Michael Burkard, "A Birthday Story." Reprinted with the permission of the author.

Jim Carroll, "Poem On My Son's Birthday" from *Fear of Dreaming: Selected Poems*. Copyright © 1993 by Jim Carroll. Reprinted with the permission of Viking Penguin, a division of Penguin Putnam Inc.

John Ciardi, "Poem for My Thirty Ninth Birthday"from *Collected Poems of John Ciardi*. Reprinted with the permission of the University of Arkansas Press.

Lucille Clifton, "the thirty eighth year" from *Good Woman: Poems and a Memoir: 1969–1980*. Copyright © 1987 by Lucille Clifton. Reprinted with the permission of BOA Editions, Ltd.

Andrei Codrescu, "Imported Days" from *Alien Candor: Selected Poems 1970–1995*. Copyright © 1995 by Andrei Codrescu. Reprinted with the permission of Black Sparrow Press.

Dennis Cooper, "John Kennedy Jr. at Twenty-one" and "For My Birthday" from *Dream Police: Selected Poems 1969–1993*. Copyright © 1995 by Dennis Cooper. Reprinted with the permission of Grove/Atlantic, Inc.

Gregory Corso, "Writ on the Eve of My 32nd Birthday" from *Long Live Man*. Copyright © 1959, 1960, 1961 by New Directions Publishing Corporation. Reprinted with the permission of the publishers.

Gregory Corso, "I Am 25" and "Birthplace Revisited" from *Gasoline and The Vestal Lady on Brattle*. Copyright © 1955, 1958 by Gregory Corso. Reprinted with the permission of City Lights Books.

Robert Creeley, "A Birthday" is reprinted from *The Collected Poems of Robert Creeley, 1945–1975*. Reprinted by permission of the University of California Press. Copyright © 1982 The Regents of The University of California.

e.e cummings, "65" Copyright © 1940 by E.E. cummings; renewed 1968 by Marion Morehouse Cummings. Reprinted from Complete Poems 1913–1962 by E.E. Cummings by permission of Harcourt Brace, Inc.

Silvia Curbelo, "Birthday Song." Reprinted with the permission of the author.

Peter Davison, "At Sixty" from *The Poems of Peter Davison*. Copyright © 1995 by Peter Davison. Reprinted with the permission of Alfred A. Knopf, a division of Random House, Inc.

Madeline DeFrees, "Birthday Poem" from *When the Sky Lets Go: Poems*. Copyright © 1978 by Madeline DeFrees. Reprinted with the permission of George Braziller, Inc.

Edwin Denby, "Birthday Sonnet" from *The Complete Poems*. Reprinted with the permission of the Estate of Edwin Denby, c/o Robert Cornfield Literary Agent, New York.

James Dickey, "The Birthday Dream" from *The Whole Motion: Collected Poems, 1945–1992*. Copyright © 1992 by James Dickey. Reprinted with the permission of Wesleyan University Press.

Diane Di Prima, "April Fool Birthday Poem for Grandpa" from *Pieces of a Dream: Selected Poems*. Copyright © 1973 by Diane Di Prima. Reprinted with the permission of City Lights Books.

Melvin Dixon, "Turning Forty in the 90's" from *Loves' Instruments* (Chicago: Tia Chucha Press, 1995). Reprinted by permission.

Rita Dove, "Wingfoot Lake" and "Turning 30, I Contemplate Students Bicycling Home" from *Selected Poems*. Copyright 8 1993 by Rita Dove. Reprinted with the permission of Rita Dove.

Alan Dugan, "A Poem for Eliot on His 90th Birthday." from *Poems 7, New and Complete Poetry. Copyright © 2000*. Reprinted with the permission of the Seven Stories Press.

Stephen Dunn, "Turning Fifty" from *New and Selected Poems 1974–1994*. Copyright 8 1994 by Stephen Dunn. Reprinted with the permission of W. W. Norton & Company, Inc.

Bob Dylan. "Forever Young" lyrics and music by Bob Dylan © 1973 Ram's Horn Music. All rights reserved and administered by Special Ryder Music. Dwarf Music.

Coleen Elroy. "At 102, Romance Comes Once A Year," from *Bone Flames*. Copyright © 1987. Reprinted with permission of Wesleyan University Press.

Edward Field." A Birthday Poem for My Little Sister" from *Counting Myself Lucky: Selected Poems 1963–1992*. Copyright © 1992 by Edward Field. Reprinted by permission of Black Sparrow Press.

Robert Fitzgerald, "Silver Age Song" from *Spring Shade: Poems 1931–1970*. Copyright 8 1971 by Robert Fitzgerald. Reprinted with the permission of New Directions Publishing Corporation.

Robert Frost, "The Birthplace" from *The Poetry of Robert Frost*, edited by Edward Connery Lathem. Copyright 8 1956 by Robert Frost, copyright 1928, 8 1969 by Henry Holt and Co. Reprinted with the permission of Henry Holt and Company, LLC.

Deborah Garrison, "She Thinks of Him On Her Birthday" from *A Working Girl Can't Win*. Copyright © 1998 by Deborah Garrison. Reprinted with the permission of Random House, Inc.

Allen Ginsberg, "Ode: My 24th Year" from *Collected Poems*. Copyright © 1984 by Allen Ginsberg. Reprinted with the permission of HarperCollins Publishers, Inc.

Louise Glück, "Birthday" from *Ararat*. Copyright © 1990 by Louise Glück. Reprinted with the permission of HarperCollins Publishers, Inc.

Ray Gonzalez, "Birthday." Reprinted with the permission of the author.

Paul Goodman, "Birthday Cake" from *The Collected Poems* (New York: Random House, 1973). Copyright © 1973 by Paul Goodman. Reprinted with the permission of Mrs. Sally Goodman.

Horace Gregory, "Early April Morning" from *Another Look*. Copyright © 1973, 1974, 1975, 1976 by Horace Gregory. Reprinted with the permission of Henry Holt and Company, LLC.

Marilyn Hacker. "To Iva, Two-And-A-Half" from *The Hand Glider's Daughter.* Copyright © 1990. Reprinted with permission of Onlywoman Press.

Michael S. Harper, "Paul Laurence Dunbar" from *Nightmare Begins Responsibility*. Copyright © 1974 by Michael S. Harper. Reprinted with the permission of the author and University of Illinois Press.

Jim Harrison, "Birthday" from *The Shape of the Journey: New and Collected Poems*. Copyright ©1998 by Jim Harrison. Reprinted with the permission of Copper Canyon Press, PO Box 271, Port Townsend, WA 98368-0271.

Robert Hayden, "October" from *Collected Poems*. Copyright ©1970 by Robert Hayden. Reprinted with the permission of Liveright Publishing Corporation.

Anthony Hecht, "A Birthday Poem" from *Collected Earlier Poems*. Copyright ©1990 by Anthony E. Hecht. Reprinted with the permission of Alfred A. Knopf, a division of Random House, Inc.

Patty Smith Hill and Mildred J. Hill, "Happy Birthday to You." Copyright © 1934 by Patty Smith Hill and Mildred J. Hill. Reprinted with the permission of Warner/Chappell, Inc. All rights reserved.

Barbara Howes, "To W. H. Auden On His Fiftieth Birthday" from *A Private Signal: Poems New and Selected*. Copyright © 1977 by Barbara Howes. Reprinted with the permission of Wesleyan University Press.

Langston Hughes, "Birth,"from *The Collected Poems of Langston Hughes*. Copyright 8 1994 by The Estate of Langston Hughes. Reprinted with the permission of Alfred A. Knopf, a division of Random House, Inc.

David Ignatow, "Birthday" from *Poems, 1934–1969*. Copyright © 1970 by David Ignatow. Reprinted with the permission of Wesleyan University Press.

Josephine Jacobsen, "The Birthday Party." Reprinted with the permission of the author.

Randall Jarrell,"Aging" from *The Complete Poems by Randall Jarrell.* Copyright © 1949, 1969 by Ms. Randall Jarrell. Copyright renewed © 1976 by Mrs. Randall Jarrell. Reprinted by permission of Farrar, Straus & Giroux, LLC.

June Jordan, "DeLiza Come to London Town, A Birthday Poem for Mark" from *Naming Our Destiny: New and Selected Poems.* Copyright © 1989 by June Jordan. Reprinted with the permission of Thunder's Mouth Press.

Donald Justice, "A Birthday Candle" from *The New Yorker* (1955). Reprinted with the permission of the author.

Maurice Kenny, "Kaherawak's Birthday" from Is Summer This Bear (Saranac Lake, NY: Chauncy Press, 1985) Reprinted with permission of the author. "For Helen, On Her 30th Birthday" reprinted with the permission of the author.

Galway Kinnell, " The First Day of the Future," from *The Past.* Copyright © 1985. Reprinted with permission of Houghton Mifflin Company, Inc.

Carolyn Kizer, "Poem for Your Birthday"from *Cool, Calm & Collected: Poems 1960–2000.* Copyright © 2001 by Carolyn Kizer. Reprinted with the permission of Copper Canyon Press, P. O. Box 271, Port Townsend, WA 98368-0271.

Etheridge Knight, "Birthday Poem" and "A Poem for a Certain Lady on Her 33rd Birthday" from *The Essential Etheridge Knight.* Copyright © 1986 by Etheridge Knight. Reprinted with the permission of the University of Pittsburgh Press.

Kenneth Koch, "Poem for My Twentieth Birthday." Reprinted with the permission of the author.

Maxine Kumin, "Birthday Poem" from *Selected Poems 1960–1990.* Copyright © 1978 by Maxine Kumin. Reprinted with the permission of W. W. Norton & Company, Inc.

Stanley Kunitz, "Passing Through" from *Collected Poems.* Copyright © 2000 by Stanley Kunitz. Reprinted with the permission of W. W. Norton & Company, Inc.

Every Day (Bolinas: Big Sky, 1975). Copyright 8 1975 by Joanne Kyger. Reprinted with the

David Lehman, "June 11" from *The Daily Mirror: A Journal in Poetry.* Copyright © 1999 by David Lehman. Reprinted with the permission of Simon & Schuster, Inc.

Brad Leithauser, "Small Waterfall: A Birthday Poem" from *Things She Did.* Copyright © 1998 by Brad Leithauser. Reprinted with the permission of Alfred A. Knopf, a division of Random House, Inc.

John Lennon, " Birthday." words and music by John Lennon and Paul McCartney. Copyright © 1968 Northern Songs.

M.L. Liebler. "Birthday Dream." Reprinted with permission by the author.

John Logan, "Lines on His Birthday" from *The Collected Poems.* Copyright© 1989 by John Logan Literary Estate, Inc. Reprinted with the permission of BOA Editions, Ltd.

Audre Lorde, "Birthday Memorial to Seventh Street" from *Collected Poems of Audre Lorde.* Copyright © 1997 by Audre Lorde. Reprinted with the permission of W. W. Norton & Company, Inc.

Robert Lowell, " Middle Age," first appeared in Life Studies. Copyright © 1956, 1959, 1960, 1961, 1962, 1963, 1964 by Robert Lowell. Reprinted from Farrar, Straus Giroux, Inc.

Cleopatra Mathis, "On a Shared Birthday" from *The Center for Cold Weather.* Reprinted with the permission of Sheep Meadow Press.

Bernadette Mayer, "Birthday Sonnet for Grace" from *Sonnets* (Tender Buttons, 1990). Copyright© 1990 by Bernadette Mayer. Reprinted with the permission of the author.

Maud Meehan, "Gift for My Mother's 90th Birthday" from *Washing the Stones: Selected Poems 1975–1995* (Paper-Machier Press, 1996). Reprinted with the permission of the author.

Samuel Menashe, "49th Birthday Trip (What Are You On?)" from *Collected Poems.* Copyright © 1986 by Saul Menashe. Reprinted with the permission of the author.

Samuel Menashe, "On My Birthday" from *The Niche Narrows: New and Selected Poems* (Jersey City: Talisman House, Publishers, 2000). Copyright© 2000 by Saul Menashe. Reprinted with the permission of the author.

W. S. Merwin, "To Donna On Her Birthday" from *Selected Poems.* Copyright 8 1988 by W. S. Merwin. Reprinted with the permission of The Wylie Agency, Inc.

Edna St. Vincent Millay, "To Jesus on His Birthday" from *Collected Sonnets.* 8 1955 by Edna St. Vincent Millay and Norma Millay Ellis. Reprinted with the permission of Elizabeth Barnett, Literary Executor.

E. Ethelbert Miller, "Edna at Seventy." from *First Light, New and Selected Poems* (Black Classic Press) Copyright © 1994. Reprinted with the permission of the author.

Vassar Miller, "On Approaching My Birthday" from *Onions and Roses.* Copyright © 1968 by Vassar Miller. Reprinted with the permission of Wesleyan University Press.

Susan Mitchell, "Havana Birth" from *Rapture: Poems.* Copyright © 1992 by Susan Mitchell. Reprinted with the permission of HarperCollins Publishers, Inc.

Paul McCartney. "Birthday" words and music by John Lennon and Paul McCartney. Copyright © 1968 Northern Songs.

James Moore, "Preparing for Fifty" from *The Long Experience of Love* (Minneapolis: Milkweed Editions, 1995). Copyright © 1995 by James Moore. Reprinted with the permission of Milkweed Editions.

Hilda Morley, "Stefan: His Birthday." Reprinted with the permission of Sheep Meadow Press.

Stanley Moss, "Poem on My Birthday." Reprinted with the permission of the author.

Lisel Mueller, "For a Thirteenth Birthday" from *Alive Together: New and Selected Poems*. Copyright © 1996 by Lisel Mueller. Reprinted with the permission of Louisiana State University Press.

Carol Muske, "Surprise" from Wyndmere. Copyright © 1985 by Carol Muske. Reprinted with permission of the University of Pittsburg Press. Also reprinted in *An Octave Above Thunder, New and Selected Poems* Copyright (s) 1997 Viking/Penguin.

Eileen Myles, "December 9th." Reprinted with the permission of the author.

Debra Nystrom, "Relic" from *A Quarter Turn*. Reprinted with the permission of Sheep Meadow Press.

Ed Ochester, "On Frank O'Hara's Birthday" and "Key West" from *The Land of Cockaigne*. Copyright © 2001 by Ed Ochester. Reprinted with the permission of Story Line Press.

Frank O'Hara," John Button Birthday, " To Canada (For Washington's Birthday," and "On a Birthday of Kenneth's," from The Collected Poems of Frank O'Hara. Copyright © 1964 by Maureen Granville-Smith, Administratrix of the Estate of Frank O'Hara.

Sharon Olds," June 24th" from *The Gold Cell* Copyright © 1989 and "Birthday Poem for My Grandmother" from *The Dead and The Living* Copyright © 1985. Reprinted with permission of Alfred A, Knopf.

Gregory Orr, "Nicole at Thirteen" from *New and Selected Poems*. Copyright © 1988 by Gregory Orr. Reprinted with the permission of Wesleyan University Press.

Alicia Ostriker, "Happy Birthday" from "A Birthday Suite" in *The Little Space: Poems Selected and New 1968–1998*. Copyright © 1998. Reprinted with the permission of the University of Pittsburgh Press.

Ron Padgett, "Poem for Joan Fagin On Her Birthday." Reprinted with the permission of the author.

Elyse Paschen," The Birth Day." Reprinted by permission of the author.

Kenneth Patchen, "What Splendid Birthdays" from *Collected Poems*. Copyright ©1968 by Kenneth Patchen. Reprinted with the permission of New Directions Publishing Corporation.

Kevin Pilkington. "Birthday" Reprinted with permission of the author.

Sylvia Plath, "A Birthday Present" from *Ariel*. Copyright © 1963 by . Reprinted with the permission of HarperCollins Publishers, Inc. and Faber & Faber, Ltd.

Stanley Plumly, "Birthday" from *Boy on the Step*. Copyright © 1989 by Stanley Plumly. Reprinted with the permission of HarperCollins Publishers, Inc.

Ishmael Reed, "The Author Reflects On His 35th Birthday" from *New and Collected Poems* (New York: Atheneum Publishers, 1980). Copyright © 1980 by Ishmael Reed. Reprinted with the permission of the author.

Liz Rosenberg, "The Birthday Party" from *Children of Paradise*. Copyright ©1993. Reprinted with the permission of the University of Pittsburgh Press.

Sonia Sanchez, "Poem at Thirty" from *Shake Loose My Skin: New and Selected Poems*. Copyright © 1999 by Sonia Sanchez. Reprinted with the permission of Beacon Press, Boston.

Philip Schultz, "For My Birthday" from *Like Wings*. Copyright 1972, 1973, 1975, 1976, 1977, 1978 by Philip Schultz. Reprinted with the permission of Viking, a division of Penguin Putnam Inc.

James Schuyler, "A Belated Birthday Poem" from *Collected Poems*. Copyright © 1993 by James Schuyler. Reprinted with the permission of Farrar, Straus & Giroux, LLC.

Karl Shapiro, "Moving In" from *The Wild Card: Selected Poems Early and Late*. Copyright © 1998 by Karl Shapiro. Reprinted with the permission of the author and the University of Illinois Press.

Charles Simic, "Birthday Star Atlas" from *Unending Blues*. Copyright © 1986 by Charles Simic. Reprinted with the permission of Harcourt, Inc.

L. E. Sissman, "Safety at Forty: or, An Abecedarian Takes a Walk" from *Night Music*. Copyright (c) 1999 by The President and Fellows of Harvard College. Reprinted with the permission of Houghton Mifflin Company. All rights reserved.

Charlie Smith, "Mother at Eighty" from *The Palms*. Copyright © 1993 by Charlie Smith. Reprinted with the permission of W. W. Norton & Company, Inc.

Patti Smith, "16 February" from *Early Work, 1970–1979*. Copyright 1994 © by Patti Smith. Reprinted with the permission of W. W. Norton & Company, Inc.

Jack Spicer, "Five Words for Joe Dunn on His 22nd Birthday" from *One Night Stand and Other Poems* (San Francisco: Grey Fox Press, 1980). Copyright © 1980 by the Estate of Jack Spicer. Reprinted with permission.

William Stafford, "The Card I Got on My Birthday Was from an Insurance Man" and "Birthday" from *Stories That Could Be True:*

Collected Poems (New York: Harper & Row, Publishers, 1977). Copyright © 1977 by William Stafford. Reprinted with the permission of the Estate of William Stafford.

Gerald Stern, "Birthday" from *This Time: New and Selected Poems*. Copyright ©1998 by Gerald Stern. Reprinted with the permission of W. W. Norton & Company, Inc.

Wallace Stevens," What We See Is What We Think" reprinted from *Collected Poems*. Copyright © 1954 by Wallace Stevens. Reprinted by permission of Alfred A. Knopf, Inc.

John Updike, "Upon the Last Day of His Forty-Ninth Year" from *Collected Poems*. Copyright © 1993 by John Updike. Reprinted with the permission of Alfred A. Knopf, a division of Random House, Inc.

Mona Van Duyn, "Birthday Card for a Psychiatrist" from *If It Be Not I: Collected Poems*. Copyright © 1992 by Mon Van Duyn. Reprinted with the permission of Alfred A. Knopf, a division of Random House, Inc.

Angelo Verga, "My Brother's Birth Day." Reprinted with the permission of the author.

Peter Viereck, "Fiftieth Birthday" from *Tide and Continuities: Last and First Poems 1995–1938*. Copyright © 1995 by Peter Viereck. Reprinted with the permission of the University of Arkansas Press.

Anne Waldman, "On Walt Whitman's Birthday." Reprinted by permission.

Robert Penn Warren, "To a Little Girl One Year Old, in a Ruined Fortress" from *The Collected Poems of Robert Penn Warren* (Baton Rouge: Louisiana State University Press, 1998). Copyright © 1985 by Robert Penn Warren. Reprinted with the permission of the William Morris Agency.

Diane Wakowski, "My Aunt Ellen Meets the Buddha on His Birthday" reprinted by permission of Black Sparrow Press.

John Weiners, "My First Midnight 49th Birthday Supper" from *Selected Poems*. Copyright © 1998 by John Weiners. Reprinted with the permission of Black Sparrow Press.

Miller Williams, "For Lucy On Her Birthday" from *Living on the Surface: New and Selected Poems*. Copyright © 1989 by Miller Williams. Reprinted with the permission of Louisiana State University Press.

William Carlos Williams, "To Be Recited to Flossie on Her Birthday" from *The Collected Poems of William Carlos Williams, Volume II, 1939–1962*, edited by Christopher MacGowan. Copyright © 1955 by William Carlos Williams. Reprinted with the permission of New Directions Publishing Corporation.

Helen Wolfert, "Birthdays." Reprinted with the permission of the author.

Nelle Wong, "Toward a 44th Birthday." Reprinted with the permission of the author.

Franz Wright, "Birthday" from *Ill Lit: Selected and New Poems.* Reprinted with the permission of Oberlin College Press.

Jay Wright, "Birthday" and "A Non-Birthday Poem for My Father" from *Transfigurations: Collected Poems* (Baton Rouge: Louisiana State University Press, 2000). Copyright © 1971 by Jay Wright. Reprinted with the permission of the author.

Paul Zweig, "Birth" from *Selected and Last Poems.* Reprinted with the permission of Wesleyan University Press.

about the editor

JASON SHINDER's books include the award winning poetry collections *Every Room We Ever Slept In*, (a New York Public Library noted book) the recently published *Among Women*, and the forthcoming *Lives of the Romantics*. He is the editor of several anthologies including, most recently, *Tales From the Couch: Writers on Therapy*, and the forthcoming *First Death: Writers on Immortality* and *What Lovest Well Remains: Conversations with Poets on Poets of the Past*. His honors include fellowships from the National Endowment for the Arts, The Yaddo Corporation, the Fine Arts Work Center in Provincetown, among others. A teacher in the graduate writing programs at Bennington College, and the New School University, he is the Founder and Director of the YMCA National Writer's Voice, YMCA of the USA Arts and Humanities, and the Director of the Writing Program at Sundance Institute.